The Scent of Freedom

A TRUE STORY OF CAPTURE AND ESCAPE DURING WORLD WAR II

ERNEST CARTER

Place of capture	Mersa Matruh, Western Desert
Place of escape	Chiavari, Italy
Date of capture	29 June 1942
Date of escape	12 September 1943
Unit	74th Field Reg. Royal Artillery 151 Brigade 50th Division 8th Army
Rank	Lance Bombardier

The Scent of Freedom

Bombardier Ernest Carter

Cover Artwork and Typeset by Shore Books, Blackborough End, Norfolk.

Printed and bound in the United Kingdom.

Contents

Preface		vii
Foreword		ix
Chapter One	Getting Ready for War	1
Chapter Two	Off to Foreign Lands	9
Chapter Three	Capture in the Desert	17
Chapter Four	Transfer to Italy	30
Chapter Five	My Bid for Freedom	40
Chapter Six	A Long Walk South	66
Chapter Seven	My Best Christmas Present	84
Chapter Eight	Back to Blighty	93

Preface

Tidying up my old desk was a task long overdue. In the first few days of retirement, I began the job of casting out all that which was no longer relevant to the new chapter in my life which was about to begin.

Delving into a mass of old household bills, mortgage statements, engineering text books and rate demands, I came upon a small black silk purse which had lain there for many years unnoticed. As I retrieved it, my thoughts raced back through the years to that day forty years ago when brave little Rosa had pressed it into my hand insisting that I would need some money. It contained several hundred lira.

For many months, Rosa had been like a mother to me and as I took my leave to walk through Italy, hoping to cross the front line and maybe even home to England, it was a relief to know that my presence with Rosa's family would no longer pose a threat. Her eyes were mist as I kissed her cheek. We knew that there was no other way.

Opening the purse, I tipped out a few jingling tarnished medals, their ribbons creased and crumpled. Among them lay a small piece of Italian marble from Carrara with two names inscribed on it in indelible ink. They were those of two young South Africans with whom I had shared part of the trek with all its hazards. Now as I look back over the years, all the events of that time seem to fall into place like a jigsaw, forming a clear and complete picture. With the passing of time there is no fading of memory and conversations of forty years ago return with clarity.

This is not a story of brave personal deeds, but rather a recalling of the unstinting hospitality and understanding I witnessed, extended to me by people in a foreign land who were supposedly our enemies. In a desperate situation, alone and scared, I found friendship and warmth. Those who helped me did so at great peril to themselves and their families. The Nazis and the Fascists were in an ugly mood. Retribution was overtaking them and the vice-like grip of war was beginning to close …

Foreword

"Once a gunner, always a gunner", the major roared at the motley group of glum faced young men in civilian clothes who comprised his audience, parading for the first time in his imposing presence.

Resplendent in the glory of the full dress uniform of an Artillery officer, he concluded his speech to welcome the new recruits into his battery, and if by those words he meant that it was to be an unforgettable experience, he was certainly right.

Press-ganged into the Territorial Army with the underlying threat of two years' military conscription, should we not enlist, we had no interest in Army life.

In our teenage years, we were only intent upon furthering our hard won careers in industry and commerce.

Jobs were hard to find in those dark days of the Depression and we had no desire to be thrown again on to the overflowing labour market.

It was quite commonplace for a young man in court before a magistrate, on some petty charge to have to choose between the Army or going to prison and this did not enhance a military career. But in the following six years we were to experience the whole gamut of emotions that war could bring.

Fear, tragedy, drama, comedy and even love.

In my own case after making a desperate break from captivity, I was to find sanctuary with the kindly people of a tiny mountain community, without whose brave and unstinted help I would not have succeeded in evading recapture and reaching safety.

This is their story …

Chapter One

Getting Ready for War

In 1928 at the age of ten I remembered an outing to Southend with my mother and brother. It was a great treat in those days, but this particular occasion was my first glimpse of the sea. I watched the distant ships sailing for the wondrous places of Kipling stories and Wizard comics, and the seeds of restlessness were sown upon me. It was not discontentment, but rather a determination to see beyond that horizon, a felling made more the intense by a painting on my classroom wall entitled "The boyhood of Raleigh". It depicted an old fisherman pointing out to sea spinning a yarn to two young boys who listened wide-eyed to his tale of adventure.

These seaside outings were wonderful; cockles and cornets and a beer for father on the Prom. We were happy despite the great depression hanging over the country. Mass unemployment and long dole queues outside the Labour Exchange. Those poor things that could not pay their rent were evicted with all their possessions piled in the gutter, and the family crying not knowing where to seek shelter. No Rent Act protection helped us in those days.

My father retired from the Post Office in 1925 due to ill health and we lived on his pension, which amounted to about two pounds a week. My mother would often pawn her rings for a few pounds just to keep us going for a while. Boshers the Pawnbrokers at the corner would always be ready to oblige. Customers would enter discreetly through a side door in case the neighbours saw them, but of course, the neighbours were doing exactly the same thing. I can remember my mother returning from the shops one day nearly in tears. She had tried to borrow a packet of tea from our local grocer, just for a few days, and had been politely refused. Ironically, the shop's name was "Charity'. She never went there again.

Poor as we were, the home was always spotless, and we always had shoes whilst many of my chums went barefoot to school. Parents could not afford to buy toys, except perhaps at Christmas when a special effort was made to give presents. We had most fun with improvised toys, our favourite being a scooter made from two pieces of wood fixed together with a ball bearing at each end for the wheels. Each rider had his own personal insignia painted on the front and we would roar around the streets challenging other gangs. These contraptions were very fast and we travelled miles on them. Some were real works of art, but to this day I do not know where the ball bearings came from.. There never seemed to be a shortage!

Real cricket bats were beyond our means, but we made our own from flat pieces of wood, roughly shaped with insulating tape round the handles. Three stumps were stuck in a wooden base and set up in the street. We had great fun until some idiot lashed out and smashed a window. The offender's father had to cough up seven shillings for the repair amid angry scenes with the occupiers. Recreation grounds seemed to be scared and "the man in the peaked cap" always cleared us off. So we played in the street until the local policeman appeared. There was no traffic then and we had the place to ourselves for games. Most of our balls were purloined from the posh people's tennis courts.

Cinemas were beginning to have their heyday. We would pool all our pennies for one of the gang to buy a ticket and when lights went down he would open the side door for the rest of us. Hidden behind a heavy curtain, we would creep in when the coast was clear. Achieving all this simply added to the fun of it all. Cowboy films with Tom Mix and Hott Gibson: Charlie Chaplin and Felix the Cat, all this with a lady banging on the piano at the base of the screen. Sometimes we would sneak upstairs to the balcony and on one occasion my friend produced a tin of sneezing powder which we puffed over the railings on to the poor people below. This was during a passionate love scene starring Rudolph Valentino. The ensuing uproar made a quick getaway expedient.

In spite of poverty of that time, people always seemed to find money for a drink. Pubs were full every evening and drunkenness quite common. Every Friday night Mrs. B. would totter down the road falling dizzily from streetlamp to streetlamp, piddling as she made her way to collapse on her doorstep. Looking back, I think that the men were trying to drown their memories of the war. Most of the fathers in the road were grim humourless men who had endured the horrors of the First World War in the trenches. They came home as conquering heroes to the "land made fit" for them, until the rigours of bad housing and no jobs shattered them, leaving them angry and bitter.

In 1926 when the General Strike came, the whole country came to a standstill. My mother sent me to Hammersmith to buy coal blocks for the fire. On reaching the Broadway, I came upon an angry mob trying to overturn an omnibus, which was trying to leave the depot. Watching spellbound, I marveled at the horror of the violence. A policewoman with a huge round helmet and a long skirt down to her feet must have spotted me. She came forward to usher me away from the terrible scene, telling me to go home. I dashed back to tell them of my great adventure, only pausing long enough to collect the coal. My comics were full of thrilling stories, but I had the real thing!

Wireless made its debut in the next few years and my eldest brother constructed a crystal set receiver. He had served in the Royal Corps of Signals during the war and had seen action at Mesopotamia fighting the Turks. My father would sit for hours with the headphones on scratching around with a cat's whisker, which had to be precisely set on the crystal, in order to receive the transmission. Occasionally he would guffaw at a funny joke. My brother and I would try to annoy him by jogging the table to bounce the whisker off. Every Armistice Day, which was then held at the proper time of the 11th November, he would listen to the Whitehall Remembrance Service with tears in his eyes. One of my brothers had been lost with Lord Kitchener on HMS Hampshire at the age of eighteen. It was his first voyage.

Eventually, we were all pushed out from school at the age of fourteen with what then passed for an education. Just as we were really beginning to learn we had to leave with no training for a profession or craft, just helping to swell the endless queues for work. After serving in a shop for several months, my restless spirit emerged and I decided to apply for the Merchant Navy, intending to become a steward on the ocean liners. I was informed, however, that uniforms and equipment would cost more than fifty pounds. This amounted to the equivalent of six months wages for an adult, a veritable fortune. I talked things over with one of my school chums and we applied to join the Royal Navy. After putting us through several tests, the Lords opined that they would be more efficient without us. The emphasis at that time was on disarmament.

Later, I was fortunate enough to be offered a job with a local firm manufacturing testing machines and scientific instruments. I settled down rapidly, feeling that I could not learn enough. At last, I had a real job, earning real money, and above all, making some good friends. The next four years were both interesting and happy – things were going well. Yet the shadow of the war began to cast itself only twenty years after the last appalling carnage. The inevitable day came when men of my age group were ordered to join either the Territorial Army or be conscripted for two years national service. I was keen on my job and enjoying life exactly the way it was. The army call up did not appeal to me. Two nights at the local drill hall would suit me. The deadline to enroll was midnight that day, and after work, I presented myself to the Royal Corps of Signals at Putney. A group of men had already arrived and the Sergeant-in-Charge informed us that they could accept no more.

Just across the road was the headquarters of the Royal Artillery Battery and that evening, they enrolled about fifty of us. A few days later we returned for a medical. It was just a quick formality, ending with the usual cough. Most of us were accepted. When I told my parents they said nothing. My brother being four years older was not affected by the call up at this time but it was only a year later when he too had to don his khaki. We tried to put my mother's mind at rest by saying that it would soon blow over …

The first night in the drill hall, and a welcoming pep talk by the major, finishing with: "One man, one job and mind your own business!" I recalled his words later when being taught the intricacies of gunnery, driving, maintenance, signaling, first aid, map-reading and infantry drill.

The constant drilling in the evenings after work eventually turned us into competent gunners. It was my first time of real discipline and I began to enjoy it. A feeling of confidence was growing in us and we began to look forward to drill nights. Our instructors were dedicated men, and although we were too young to realise it, they were the backbone to the services. Where would we have been without their specialist knowledge? I recall one tubby little sergeant in particular who bellowed in my ear "When you get an order, you don't walk, you don't run, you flyee!!"

We were issued with uniform, which at that time was full riding kit, boots spurs, breeches and brass buttons. Battle dress had not yet appeared and a few units still had their horses. I toyed with the idea of transferring to "K" Battery, the smart ceremonial gunners who fired all the royal salutes. The artillery maintained a very high degree of smartness. Guns and vehicles had to be spotless for Saturday inspection. Spade and pick handles were glass papered and all metal parts were polished. Proudly returning home with my kit, my father looked sad. He had seen it all before and had already lost one dear son in 1916. My mother simply said "bloody Germans".

Summer came and we were packed off to a practice firing camp in North Wales, high in the mountains at Trawsfyndd. My employer stopped my wages for these two weeks, remarking, by way of consolation, "it was good fun". Army pay of fourteen shillings weekly was not much fun. My parents needed those wages. It rained most of the time, but at least we learnt how to pitch tents in a downpour. The food, however, was appalling and dissatisfaction led to a mass boycott at meal times. Many of us went to a local café to make our resentment known, and being subsequently late for parade caused an uproar. Promises were made that things would improve and that we were asked to bear in mind that cooking staff were also training for the task of mass feeding. Conditions began to improve with the introduction of "Gunfire" first thing in the morning. This was a bucket of piping hot tea brought to each tent. Our morale began to pick up.

Rain or shine, we continued to drill daily and the boggy terrain made it difficult to handle the guns although they had large wagon wheels. It proved to be excellent training. It was the second week, which brought our baptism of real gunfire. We were now dealing with live ammunition. Kneeling to attention by the side of an eighteen pounder, I was in the loading position. A shell was passed to me from behind as we had done so many times in training. The brass nose cover had been removed and the firing pin exposed. I expected it to explode at any minute, my spine tingling all of the time. Really it was quite safe. A metal tape was wound round under the head of the dreaded pin and this uncoiled after the shell had left the barrel. This type of ammunition was in one piece like a huge bullet. The breach was open, and when the command came to load, I rammed the shell home with a tightly clenched fist. I awaited the order, "fire", in trepidation, totally unprepared for the earthquake that followed. With a churning, thunderous roar, the gun reared like a wild horse. The barrel recoiled with a thud, missing my face by inches. I felt sick, deafened: my head was bursting. The breech was open again and the brass cartridge shot out with a clang. Another round was being pushed under my arm. We were told to open our mouths to lessen the shock for the second round. It was quite an experience, but we gradually became inured to it.

By now the Germans were threatening Poland. Czechoslovakia had already fallen and the fires of war were steadily flickering. Early in September 1939 mobilisation began. I received a telegram whilst at work informing me that I should report "not later than immediately". I collected my wages and returned home for a quick meal. When I donned my uniform my father was silent and I knew his thoughts.

The following day, the Battery left for Golders Green and civilian billets. The owners of many of the houses had expected a blitz and had evacuated to safer areas. Their property was requisitioned for military use. The first air raid warning came as Britain declared war. We were parading in the street at the time and looked up at the sound of the sirens. Our Sergeant Major ordered us to look to the front saying, "Don't look up men, you will frighten the civilians". Never mind the civilians, the Sergeant Major himself frightened us. He was a huge man with a waxed moustache and a face like leather, his voice audible for ten miles at least!

Before the Battery moved off to Canterbury for field training, I slipped home to see my family. It was against the rules but it would be six months before I would see them again. The British army was retreating from France through Dunkirk and the outlook was looking grim. Expecting the Germans to follow with a full-scale invasion, we set up a gun position in an old Roman Castle overlooking Sandwich. Patrolling round the castle walls at night was quite eerie, visualising the old Roman centurions.

Two weeks later I was transferred to a Brigade in Dorset, which had been badly battered in France. They had fought a brave rear guard action and halted the enemy allowing the escaping troops more time. This was the famous 50th Division from Northumberland. They were tough men who had worked in the coalmines and shipyards. They had lived through the Great Depression around Jarrow. Their stories of the distress of those days made my childhood seem quite rosy by comparison. They were rough and ready men, their Geordie accents hard to understand, but they were excellent soldiers and good-hearted comrades. They shared all they had and I made good friends among them. I was always addressed as Carter EEEE at roll call, and they all assumed that my name was Edward. Despite my protests the name stuck and I became "Eddie" for the duration.

We had no equipment and slept rough in a large marquee pitched in a field near Dorchester, huddling close together. One night I dreamed that I had lost my identity disc from around my neck. Groping around in the dark, my fingers passed over the man next to me. He let out a fearful scream, yelling that a rat had crossed his face. His shouts alarmed everyone else and the men thought that the invasion had begun. In the panic I kept quiet, realising it was me who had caused the uproar.

We were soon to be re-equipped and to our surprise we were presented with six old French guns. The famous 75s mm. We laughed, wondering where they had raked these out. Compared with British guns they were crude and ugly. The sights were simple, not the precision instruments we were accustomed to. However, we soon became accustomed to them and realized how good they were, very quick firing with a good crew, and more important still, rugged and reliable. Taking up position in the hills, we ranged on the beach at Abbotsbury and awaited the German invaders.

With the advancing winter, however, the threat of invasion passed. The French guns were sent away and the Battery headed for Tiverton in Devon. My troop was billeted in an ancient college named "Old Blundells". It was great to be back in town after so long in the field.

Many weeks of intense training on Exmoor licked us into shape and we were ready for action overseas. Rumours began to circulate. Someone had seen a tropical kit being delivered to the stores. About this time, a fresh-faced young officer, 2nd Lieutenant Poole-Hughes, joined us. We understood that he was training to be a minister of the Church in civilian life and we would try not to swear when he was around. His cheeks would flush when he heard bad language, but he was greatly respected and his quiet efficiency made him popular with everyone. The ability that he had with mathematics and trigonometry was badly needed to improve our gunnery. Field guns hit their targets with careful calculation. Many months later he was taken prisoner after the fall of Tobruk. He escaped from a prison camp in Italy and walked down through the enemy lines to rejoin the Regiment. Taking part in the invasion of Normandy he was wounded and after recovering, rejoined the unit only to suffer another wound at Nijmegen. He was a most courageous officer with an outstanding record. At the time of writing he is now the Bishop of Llandaff near Cardiff.

It was whilst dancing in Tiverton one evening with a pleasant girl whose company I had enjoyed for several weeks, that I was told our regiment would be leaving soon for Egypt. Two weeks later, we were sailing down the Clyde on the Duchess of Bedford, only to run aground on a sandbank. Two thousand men had to be disembarked on a fleet of barges and were marched round the dock area until the ship was refloated. When we arrived at this port of embarkation, we were quite surprised to find that a strike was in progress, and the dockers had withdrawn their labour. The army had to load all of the lorries and equipment. This was unbelievable at a time when Britain had her back to the wall and was fighting alone.

Chapter Two

Off to Foreign Lands

We eventually set sail, however and zigzagging our way down to the Equator, we were put all through the rites of crossing the line and given Father Neptune's Certificate. After a six week journey, we arrived in Suez where we remained for two weeks to accustom ourselves to the heat. Our next port of call was Cyprus and the Navy shipped us across and unloaded at lightening speed. The harbour was constantly under attack from the air. Crete had fallen to the Germans and Cyprus would be next, it seemed. During the following weeks, strong points were set up and guns ranged on the airfield near the capital. We continued to train in the pleasant countryside until the threat of invasion had passed. The Brigade was then moved to Palestine and then in convoy for a long journey to the Russian border in Northern Iraq. The German army was advancing towards the Caucasus Mountains and Stalin's forces were on the retreat. This posed a threat to the oilfields of Iraq and Iran. The Division had been ordered up to the border with the intention of going in to fight with the Russians, but on arrival, only the guns and the lorries were wanted, not the troops. They would not entertain the idea of British soldiers on their territory however sorely pressed. On the way through Iraq, we witnessed a dreadful spectacle. An Iraqi gun Battery had been attacked from the air. Dead horses and overturned guns covered a wide area. It was a tragic sight.

Our preparation for action began in the Western Desert. Vehicles and guns were painted to match the sand and we received more equipment. This was obviously going to be the real thing. Driving out through Egypt, we took over a defensive position from an Indian Brigade at Gazala near Tobruk. I was part of an observation crew, patrolling in a radio truck to keep a check on enemy activity. On one of our patrols, we captured a water tanker heading for German lines. This was a great prize and was returned to our side under escort.

It was whilst on duty at a forward observation post one day that a large group of enemy infantry advanced towards us. In this instance the Captain dispersed them with gunfire, but later in the afternoon, we heard the sound of a vehicle directly in front of us among the dunes. The Captain went forward to investigate. Time passed by and we became anxious by his long absence. The radio operator and I went forward to search. There was no trace of him, just an eerie silence. Of course, we had to inform the gun position of his disappearance, and so another Officer arrived to take his place. It was Lieutenant Poole-Hughes.

Around midday, the scorching heat made observation almost impossible. The desert landscape vanished in a shimmering haze, so sickeningly hot you could almost breathe it in. Welcome relief would only come in the relative cool of the late afternoon and evening. In the absence of shade, tins of petrol would balloon outwards under the pressure of the heat. The vehicles them selves were too hot to touch and we all used to dream of iced drinks in Cairo. In the intensity of the sun, it was almost impossible to eat anything without a drink and each vehicle possessed its own stove for brewing up – improvised of course. It consisted of a tin of sand mixed with almost half a gallon of petrol and this concoction would burn for some time. In the darkness and the cool of the evening, little fires would blossom out like water lilies. Sometimes I think that more petrol was burnt for making tea than was used in driving the trucks! In times of crisis the tranquilising effect of a warm drink was wonderful.

One day we were relieved from observation duty and returned to the gun position for a rest and a clean up. Our place was taken by three others, one of them being my friend Jim. He was a London man like myself and we had become pals during our desert service. It was several hours later when we returned to find Jim and the others talking excitedly. Jim stood by the radio truck pointing to a steel water tank on top. He had been sitting on the tank during observation and an armour piercing shell had actually passed between his legs, through the tank and narrowly missed the radio operator. He had been wearing headphones at the time and had been quite unaware of the incident. Their faces were blanched white. It had shaken them badly. Twelve inches higher and Jim would have been hit. The hole in the tank was just less than two inches in diameter. It was fortunate that it had not been an explosive shell.

Some weeks later, we again had a narrow escape. Going forward after dark in a Bren Carrier, we set up an observation post on the hillside near a section of the Durham Light Infantry. There was a dugout. It was very quiet and we all settled down. Then, without warning, the whole front seemed to open up at us in a hail of bullets and mortar fire. Tracers were screaming all around and we were baffled as to how they could see us in the dark when a furious Infantry Officer raced up and yelled at us to get off the skyline. Looking behind, we realized that an immense full moon had risen over the horizon and we were silhouetted right in the middle. Even before the driver could start the engine, there came a dull thud and the Carrier shuddered deeply. We had been hit. An armour piercing shell had penetrated the thin metal of the vehicle, slicing off the gear lever at ground level. The driver had been hit in the eye and we pulled him clear of the vehicle, taking cover behind the hill. The darkness deepened and the firing died away. We fixed up a make shift tent to examine the driver's eye. It was bleeding profusely. The Officer applied a field dressing to patch him up temporarily and we radioed the gun position. A party was despatched to recover the stricken Carrier and we returned for a replacement vehicle.

One morning, in the course of our roving observation duties, we advanced to what was thought to be safe territory only to be greeted by a burst of gunfire. To our dismay, the enemy had moved forward some considerable distance from their previous position during the night. This kind of information had to be relayed back quickly in a situation report. We did not realise at the time, but this was the prelude to Rommel's assault on Tobruk.

Only days later, the German armour advanced. To our left flank another Brigade of the 50th Division was under attack. Thick columns of black smoke filled the sky with the thunderous noise of the Panzers. The Brigade was trying to desperately to resist the onslaught of the Africa Corps. While the battle raged, we waited tensely for our turn to come under fire. It was during the afternoon that we had the devastating news that Rommel had taken the Garrison of Tobruk. The South Africa Division in occupation had surrendered. We later heard that thirty thousand men had been taken prisoner.

Tobruk had been our anchor and stay. Months previously, British and Australian troops had held out against repeated assaults on their positions. Now with our line breached on the coast, the Panzers swept through unhindered. With another enemy column approaching from deep in the desert, we were surrounded and trapped. We awaited our orders – someone had to make a decision. With evening approaching the order came after dark an attempt would be made to break out through the enemy line. Each unit was to make it back to Mersa Matruh. The Eighth Army was in complete disarray and on the retreat.

Shortly after dark, the convoy started off, trundling towards the east. Things seemed to be going pretty well. And we could scarcely believe our luck when suddenly a lorry in front of us erupted in a mass of flames. Others were exploding round us. We were in the middle of a minefield and there was no turning back. The men were shouting and running, flitting like shadows in the nightmarish orange of the flames. The German tanks in the distance were immediately alerted and they opened fire, adding to the devastation. We kept our heads down in the Carrier, the steel walls protecting us from flying splinters. Our luck held out as we kept going, and we reached comparative safety.

Looking back we saw a grim sight. The scene was of burning vehicles and more explosions, but our own Guardian Angel must have stayed with us through that perilous time. Several hours later as the dawn broke, the desert sands were a mass of vehicles and men on foot, making their way to the rear. We were just glad to have come through unscathed.

On reaching the outskirts of Mersa Matruh, we found that a defensive line was being established. After a short rest and a quick meal, all drivers were ordered to parade, and then informed that we would be going back. A vehicle depot had been abandoned at Buq-Buq some seventy miles away and a race against time began to retrieve as many trucks as possible before the Africa Corps could seize them. We set out in four lorries at breakneck speed back in the face of the advancing enemy. It seemed that we were tempting fate once again. Several drivers had arrived at the dump before us and the vehicles began to stream out in convoy. The Officer in charge allocated a truck to each of us and after quickly checking the oil, water and fuel, we began the return journey. I had been given a small lorry and we drove off into the desert, trying to avoid the coastal road.

The salvage attempt seemed to be going quite well – until my engine began to splutter and cough. After a while, it stopped altogether and I pulled over allowing the other trucks to pass on. I fully expected someone to stop and enquire if help were needed and was surprised when the end of the column flashed past and they all vanished into the distance. On normal convoys, a fitter always brought up the rear, but this was not a normal convoy. Left to figure things out for myself, I decided to clean the fuel pump filter. I extracted the pipe and blew through it to make sure that it was not blocked and then tried the starter, the engine absolutely refused to fire. With a silent prayer, I removed the distributor cover to check the spark, when without warning; a roar and an explosion just a few yards away deafened me. I grabbed the distributor cover, poured a handful of sand in the oil filter for good measure, and raced away to the cover of the dunes. Several more rounds followed my departure.

I headed in a southerly direction and as the day wore on, I began to feel the effects of the blistering heat. Turning east I walked in the direction of Mersa. A few miles further on, I looked over my soldier and saw a vehicle approaching through the rippling heat. Concealed behind a small hill, I intended to remain hidden had the lorry been German, but fortunately it was a British three-tonner. A Sergeant drove it with two other men and all were from the 50th Division. Most welcome of all was the plentiful supply of water they had on board and we all relished a long drink. Two Geordies among the company pulled out a battered old portable gramophone with just one record – Bobbie Breene singing "Rainbow on the River" – and we sailed on through the desert to wafting strains of this song.

When he discovered that I was a driver, the Sergeant asked me to take the wheel for a while. Several miles further along through the sands, we spotted two distant figures trudging along. These men were black soldiers who had been with the South Africans and at the fall of Tobruk had escaped with several others. Now they had been separated and after walking for nearly two days without a drop of water to share, they were exhausted. Only their determination had kept them going. We offered them a drink and a rest and they swiftly revived saying that they were frightened of the prospect of being captured by the Germans.

Still further along, we made another amazing discovery: a huge divisional food dump about one hundred yards square, surrounded by a high barbed wire fence. The gates were wide open and the place completely abandoned. It was a veritable treasure trove: crates of food piled twelve feet high, food of every description, everything to keep the Eighth Army on its feet. Of course, we eagerly stocked up with tins of peaches and milk and a mass of army issue cigarettes. No attempt had been made to destroy the place and stop the enemy taking possession. It would have a great prize for them but there was no time for us to think of sabotage. Months later, starving in a Benghazi prison camp, we were to be tormented by thoughts of all that food.

We continued our journey through the desert, all eating peaches and milk. Our two black friends seemed to be enjoying it all and a sense of bonhomie and ease settled over us. Surely all this was too good to last. And of course, as if it were foreordained, a few miles further on we hit soft sand and the rear wheels of the truck dug in. It was lucky that we had plenty of experience with this problem and we commenced digging channels in front of each wheel straight away. We laid down blankets and brushwood to enable the tyres to gain some purchase on the ground. All of these activities were carried out to the wafting strains of Bobbie Breene and his Rainbow, our stomachs filled with peaches and milk.

It was not long before we heard the creaking and clattering of tanks in a valley to our left. Fortunately, we were obscured from their view for the time being. Very cautiously, we climbed to the brow of the dune and observed a column of armour moving to the north away from us. With great relief, we watched them gradually disappear and sighing, we returned to the task of freeing the truck. The Sergeant seemed confident about the route we were to take and when we successfully freed the vehicle, we continued deeper into the desert. Some way further on, we found a hard track and turned eastwards.

As evening drew on, I suggested that we stop for the night: driving was hazardous after dark and the truck could be easily disabled in a rut or hole. But the Sergeant wanted to push on and we therefore proceeded carefully. Soon, a large dark image appeared before us and we approached at the lowest speed. Peering into the darkness, it seemed to be a gun position and shadowy figures were standing around. One of these figures detached themselves and started walking towards us. As his face almost touched mine, I realized with horror that he was a German. He was not sure about us and did not speak. I yanked the wheel whilst the Sergeant yelled for us to run for it and raced off into the darkness. Rifle shots and general commotion followed us.

We fled at some considerable speed and when at last we reached a safe distance, we slowed down and decided to stop until first light. We all had a drink and laughed about our close shave, wondering which side had received the greater shock. As dawn broke, we looked around with the field glasses. There was no apparent movement so we started off, fairly confident that the front line could not be far away, but it seemed very quiet.

Before long, our unbroken stretch of moderate good fortune ran out and a burst of machine gun fire tore across our path. It was a direct challenge to halt. To have made a run for it would have meant disaster for we were a sitting target. We stopped the truck and ran for a gully, which gave us some cover. I spotted some gorse to my right and made my way to it, keeping low all the time. The others disappeared in the dunes. Expecting a patrol to search for us, I kept going hoping to meet up with the others at some stage.

Later in the afternoon, I found a sheltered spot and rested until dark. Luckily, I still had my haversack with me containing my water bottle. Walking at night could have been dangerous, and after the events of the past day, I decided not to take a risk. It was chilly after the heat of the day, but I took a welcome rest. In the morning, my clothes were wet and uncomfortable. I had a drink and a smoke and climbed to the top of the hill for a look around. I still possessed my compass and binoculars, and seeing no movement elsewhere, I set off to the south with the intention of swinging round later to reach our lines.

Chapter Three

Capture in the Desert

As the heat intensified I walked on, confident that I had reached safety. A young Africa Corps soldier suddenly confronted me. He sprang out of his foxhole and his machine gun pointing directly at me. He motioned me to raise my hands. There was no menace in his face, in fact he was smiling and pleasant, not at all what I expected. He asked if I had any cigarettes and I offered my packet. He took one and thanked me before handing the rest back. Taking my binoculars and compass, he casually informed me that I would not be requiring them any longer as my war was over. Like a bolt from the blue, I realised I was now a prisoner of war.

The young Africa Corps soldier and I were about the same size, and he was lightly built. As we smoked, I weighed up the likelihood of overpowering him and getting away, but common sense told me that he was not alone. Pointing to a position some hundred yards away, he told me that I would find some of my friends, and as I walked away a group of Germans appeared from a dip in the ground and waved me over. They had obviously been watching the proceedings. I was glad I had not tried to make a break for it. Beyond them, a group of men were sitting on the ground surrounded by guards. All these were Eighth Army men who had been roped in while struggling back, trying to reach safety. Among them I found the Sergeant and four others from the truck and after talking over previous events, it was agreed that stopping when we did was the only choice, and to drive away would probably have caused casualties among us.

After so many months of action during which both sides had been trying their hardest to slaughter each other, coming face to face with the enemy like that was an overwhelming experience. At first a feeling of great relief comes when the realisation that you have escaped injury dawns. Only when hearing those words "for you the war is over" does the reality of the situation become clear. You are no longer part of the opposition, no longer a combatant. From that moment on, you must be afforded shelter, safety, provided for under the protection of the Geneva Convention, which supposedly governs the rules of warfare. Of course, all this is not instantly possible, being secondary to the conditions prevailing at the time. You have been disarmed and neutralised, another name to be listed as missing with the Red Cross.

The initial shock and relief quickly fade, followed by a sense of complete degradation: a feeling that you have failed in your duty, you have let the side down! All of the training had been to no avail, a waste! I wondered how my family would take the news that I was missing in action. These thoughts flashed through my mind and I supposed that other men must be feeling the same. When this trauma had begun to sink in, feelings took an upward turn. At least I had survived and may live to fight another day. Escape had been uppermost in my thoughts, to get away before being transported to the rear. My regiment was so close, just a few miles across the hills. Searching for a way out pushed to the feelings of recrimination. For the duration of my captivity, the challenge to win freedom was never subdued.

As evening came, a salvo of British twenty-five pounder shells screeched over to burst about two hundred yards away. I had often wondered what it was like to be on the receiving end of our guns and now I was getting first hand experience. It was not very pleasant, and my belief that we were right on the front line was confirmed. With the setting sun behind us, I thought of the time we had been caught in the moonrise. We all managed to laugh at the irony of the situation to think that we could be killed by our own side. But the gunfire was short-lived and we were thankful when it ended.

Soon, a German Officer approached our group, informing us that we would be taken to safety as soon as transport could be arranged. He apologised for the lack of drinking water and assured us that he would do his best to provide it. He returned some time later with a party of men carrying containers. We had a drink and those with bottles were allowed to replenish them. At the same time he ordered us to be closely herded together. Apparently there were no vehicles to move us and we would have to remain until the following day. This was indeed good news. Perhaps there would be the chance to slide off into the darkness of the early hours. The German walked among us, chatting here and there in English. Seeing our two black companions, he seemed to be quite concerned that they had nothing with which to cover themselves. It was beginning to get chilly. Some of the prisoners seem to have held on to their great coats and several had blankets. He endeavoured to borrow something warm for "these poor little black boys". We settled down for the night. A ring of sentries was posted, surrounding the huddled group and a machine gun set up to cover the whole scene. A gap of some twenty feet separated the troops from the prisoners and as luck would have it, the visibility was quite good causing any movement to be instantly seen. There was no way to cross that belt unobserved.

At first light, we were roused and marched to the rear for about a mile where a small convoy of lorries was waiting. Even at this moment we were still hoping for deliverance, perhaps a commando raid, perhaps our tanks breaking through, but nothing! Our spirits sunk as we boarded the trucks. Two guards sat at the tailboards. The convoy drove north to the coast road and Tobruk, a journey of about a hundred and fifty miles. Driving along the tarmac road, the blue Mediterranean was about a hundred yards away. It was beautiful to see after months in the desert.

We were occasionally allowed breaks during the journey. Some of us felt sick with the exhaust fumes which filled the truck. During one of the halts, the German Officer invited all of us to go for a swim.. This was very welcome and the morning was still cool. Stripping off naked on the beach, we saw a machine gun being set up on a high ground behind us. We had grave misgivings about this as a burst of machine gun fire came over our heads. It served to test the weapon and frighten us, but our fears were allayed to some extent when a party of naked Germans plunged in beside us laughing. Everyone enjoyed the pleasant interlude, and we thanked the Africa Corps Officer for his thoughtfulness.

There was still no sign of food, however, and it seemed that no one felt hungry. Water was the most important thing. During one of our roadside breaks, a German convoy halted alongside us. The troops all looked clean and smart with guns and vehicles freshly painted. All this gave the impression that new forces were arriving in the desert. On the sides of the tanks and trucks was the Palm Tree Insignia of Rommel's Africa Corps. They all had a calm air of efficiency about them. Either side showed no open hostility. Quiet curiosity was more in evidence than anything else. No one spoke. After they had moved on, someone quipped, "for us the war is over, but for them it is just beginning".

There was a marked difference when a convoy of Mussolini's troops passed on their way to the front. They greeted us with a chorus of jeers and we responded in like fashion. The Bersaglieri with black feathers on their helmets received a particular torrent of abuse.

When at last we came to Tobruk, we were all feeling the enervating effects of the long, hot journey. This was June and although being quite close to the sea, it was pretty warm. At the outskirts we were handed over to the Italians and marched to a prison compound formed by a large circle of coiled barbed wire. The cage was about fifty yards across, and as we arrived, the prisoners already there came to greet us. I saw some familiar faces of several men from our Battery, and that of my old friend Jim. Later, we all exchanged details leading up to our capture. Before being allowed to mix with the others, we lined up to be searched. Details of name, rank and number were all that was demanded in the way of information. Our meager possessions were thoroughly investigated and anything that could prove useful in an escape attempt was removed. An army steel dinner knife was in my haversack and I slipped it into my boot, thereby managing to keep possession of it. I thought it might prove useful.

It was while this process was going on that a nasty incident took place when an Italian guard demanded the wristwatch from a tall South African. The man refused to hand it over, telling the guard what to do in no uncertain terms. At this the soldier spat in his face and the South African lunged forward, fists raised and eyes ablaze with anger. Only the intervention of a German officer prevented bloodshed. In all fairness this was the only time that such an incident occurred and we understood later that the Italian soldier had been reprimanded for his conduct.

Before joining the other men, we were all issued with a huge dry biscuit about one inch thick and five inches square. It seemed to consist of flour and water baked very hard, and it was quite tasteless. At least it was something to chew. We were told it was standard Italian army issue. Over the next months we were to become acquainted with real hunger: hunger so intense that men who had been perfect specimens of physical fitness when taken prisoner could no longer find the strength to walk across the compound.

A short distance away, we could see an airfield, and what appeared to be German fighter planes. The talk inevitably turned to escape and even the idea of stealing an aircraft was considered. Some of the men were confident they could handle it, but the greatest problem would be the initial starting of the engine. For the time being, escape plans remained unformed.

The sanitary arrangements within the compound were virtually non-existent apart from the hole in the sand at one end, and there were no means with which to wash ourselves. This was only a transit camp and two days later a convoy of trucks arrived to transport us to Benghazi and six months of privation.

These were open lorries so we had no problems with exhaust fumes choking us back. It took most of the day to cover the two hundred and fifty miles to Benghazi and we were well guarded during our breaks at the roadside. Escape was out of the question. There was no cover at all to slip into.

On arriving at our destination, we saw that the camp was a much more permanent affair than the previous one. A huge square, surrounded by a double barbed wire fence, eight feet high with guards at regular intervals. Hundreds of prisoners of different nationalities were milling around. The Eighth Army was a very mixed crowd. Many of them waited by the gate as we entered the camp, they were hoping to get a glimpse of a friend or to get any news of the progress of the war. This was a regular thing when a new batch of prisoners arrived, and we soon found ourselves doing the same thing. A large number of bivouac tents had been set up, housing six prisoners in each. They were not high enough to stand up in but at least provided shelter from the scorching heat, which was to become more intense during the next few weeks.

We were delighted to discover a washhouse at one corner of the camp with running cold water and several showers. After a good scrub and shave, we felt much better and at last I could change my socks and wash the old pair. When water was scarce in the desert we had been used to washing our socks in petrol! All this cleanliness, however, only seemed to increase the pangs of hunger. The latrines were the usual crude affair, a trench surmounted by a long wooden pole, which creaked ominously when fully loaded. All self-consciousness had long since evaporated, even from the most modest among us. So many of the men were suffering the dire effects of dysentery and the only medication available to them was Epsom Salts. They were told that the stuff would help their condition, but they were all in a very bad way. I was unusual in that I did not suffer at all from this scourge.

At midday, a small truck entered the camp, causing a flurry of activity in all directions. Men appeared from their tents and gathered in groups, a motley crew of many differing nations; Aussies and New Zealanders in broad hats, a few Ghurkas, Indians in turbans and South Africans in their distinctive sun helmets and smart brown leather boots, which had always been the envy of the British Tommy. I noticed a number of Free French soldiers who had fought so bravely at Bir Hacheim when attacked by Rommel's armour at the extreme end of our line deep in the desert. The fall of Tobruk had been a disaster for them too. Several distribution points were set up and our NCOs told us which queue to join. Loaves of bread were collected in blankets from the lorry for each group and were handed to us, as we filed past. It was about the size of a fist, dark brown and doughy in texture. As newcomers, we stood around nibbling our bread and watching the proceedings with some interest. We saw that some of the men had put their loaves inside their shirts. At the end of this ritual, we were quite unprepared for what followed. The blanket was picked up and shaken, scattering crumbs and bits of broken bread into the sand. The prisoners who had been waiting made a mad scramble among the sand for the tiny morsels. We watched this sight with amazement and surprise. Surely men had not been reduced to this?

It was to become such a familiar sight each day that we eventually took no notice.

We spoke to some of the men who had been in this camp for several weeks, enquiring when the next food would be forthcoming and were told that we had been given our ration for the day. The next bread would be issued at the same time the following day. We were absolutely shocked. Surely this could not be the whole ration for the next twenty-four hours. But this was the disheartening truth and was to be so for the next six months. Just bread and water. When bread was not available, we had one of the Italian dry biscuits. Maybe twice monthly, a small tin of meat was provided weighing about four ounces in total. We had expected a hard time before we arrived at this place but had hoped for something better from an organised camp of this size.

Frequent deputations were made to the German commander and always met with the same response: it was the naval blockade and we were getting the same as the troops in the field. We found this very hard to believe but were constrained to believe it as the only explanation offered.

The Indian prisoners collected and distributed their own particular food. Whether they fared better than us was debatable but they seemed to be issued with a rice and a type of butter from buffalo fat which they cooked on little fires outside their tents. An exotic aroma of cooking oil mingled with the fragrant smoke from burning cedar wood drifted through our lines every day as though to torment us. We passed the time with a grisly game called "Dinners'. One would draw a circular plate in the sand, and we all added something of our choice such as a piece of roast beef or Yorkshire pudding. When the plate was full it was started again with a fresh menu. I recalled the huge food dump that we had found and the poor men listened with interest. It was terrible to think of that massive store falling into enemy hands. Those of us who had managed to retain our haversacks through thick and thin still had our army emergency rations. This was a sealed tin of plain chocolate about one inch thick, supposed containing all the nourishment to sustain life for a while. It was the standard military issue and being part of our kit was inspected at regular intervals. To tamper with this was to commit the unforgiveable, almost treasonable in fact, and one could imagine the court martial and firing squad, "In that you did consume your emergency ration". I often wondered what would happen when ten million of these were returned to the Quartermaster general. We had never seen the contents and decided this was emergency enough to suffer the privation of bread and water for so long. Expecting the heavens to fall upon us, one of the tins was unsealed and the contents sampled. It was very hard and dry, which increased out thirst, but it, was something to chew and gave our flagging morale a boost. We needed something to cling to in those terrible months when we were so low and the news of the war was sketchy and scarce.

In the showers one morning, I met another prisoner from my regiment and he informed me that our signals sergeant had been wounded in the retreat, quite seriously in fact. He was one of those unforgettable characters that one meets from time to time, a small man with a permanent grin on his wrinkled face. He was like a little gnome, and very efficient with his signaling equipment. All through our travels he had kept a huge guitar with him, almost as big as himself, and it took pride of place when we packed up to move on. At every opportunity when things were quiet, he would tune up and sing cowboy songs. It was always pleasant to hear and we were sorry to hear this sad news of his wounding.

Another of these unforgettable characters had been the Medical Corps Dentist. For several weeks, I had been troubled with a slight toothache, and it had gradually progressed to one of those searing, throbbing pains, which drives all other thoughts from your mind. Reporting sick, I had visions of seeing some kind of civilisation for a few hours away from the desert fighting. I travelled back through the lines with others suffering ailments and we eventually pulled into a Medical corps camp. To my surprise they had a dental surgery in the back of a large lorry. The Dentist was a huge man, stripped to the waste and sweating profusely. He dealt with my red-hot tooth before I had time to think about it, to my immense relief. So much for all of my dreams of civilization.

But now, in the prison camp, these people seemed to belong to another lifetime. Our only concerns were how to survive the powerful hunger of the next day. Pre-captivity memories reminded us of a life which seemed very far away indeed. Every morning large numbers of men gathered at the gate to go on working parties to the Benghazi docks. They were all volunteers and were apparently unloading enemy supply ships. British prisoners were forbidden by the camp Sergeant Major to join these expeditions. Obviously, it was helping the Nazi's war effort and caused much bad feeling. We had no jurisdiction over the others and they went out each day returning in the evening to run our gauntlet of boos and jeers. Sometimes stones were thrown in anger. They had usually scrounged while they were out, dates or potatoes. Occasionally it was apples or oranges and all this increased the animosity.

As the weeks dragged on, we all bartered anything of value in our possession with the guards outside the wire. This happened all of the time as the hunger increased. Showing a sentry my wristwatch, he offered two small loaves, which I accepted. Wrapping my watch in my towel, I tossed it over the barbed wire. After making sure it was still ticking, he took two loaves from his tunic and tossed them across to me. Strangely enough in all these transactions there never seemed to be any deliberate swindling and if the goods were not up to expectation they were returned for further bargaining. Honour among thieves! All this was strictly forbidden, of course, and if the guards were caught, they were punished.

As in all camps of this type, cigarettes became the main currency. We were issued with a few Italian Nationale cigarettes each week and the Australians set up a gambling game called "Two up". A large circle was formed and each punter placed a cigarette in front of him. The bookie covered his bet with another and two coins were tossed. Head you win, tails it was theirs. It was good entertainment and possible to win quite a few if your luck was in.

Boredom was a major factor in the camp, and impromptu concerts were arranged outside the administration tent and at the same time we were given any news available about the war. There were some fine singers and for a while we drowned our sorrows in a singsong. It was here that I first became acquainted with the lovely "Lile-Marlene". I could never understand why we sang it to a German marching song, but it was brimming with drama and nostalgia and became very popular. We heard it in German, English, French and Italian – and wailing Arabic. Even the Indians had their own versions.

One night, a commando raid on Benghazi caused some excitement and we had visions of being liberated. It was only a few miles away and we felt pretty sure that they would take the camp. Our spirits sank as the firing died away without any sign of the raiders coming our way. Three months dragged on and hunger was taking its toll. Our condition had deteriorated to such an extent that it was difficult to muster enough strength to walk. The strolls round the camp had to be abandoned. Our legs would no longer support us for any great distance and we sat most of the time. Morale plummeted and there was a complete absence of any attempt at humour. It was an effort to even think and the once bustling camp was wrapped in a strained silence. Anything of value had long since gone over the wire for bread. Our excellent fitness at the time of capture had stood us in good stead so far but the lack of vitamins was sapping our strength and several men were removed for hospital treatment. We were all very thin and bony and still existed on bread and water. Jim was suffering from dysentery and looked very ill. I somehow escaped the ravages of this illness.

I had my own problems however. An old gash in my hand began to fester and the foul smell attracted a multitude of enormous flies. Even after I bound it with a field dressing which I had managed to retain, they still persisted.

Through all this time, it had still not been possible to write home to comfort our relatives and we considered that they would probably have thought the worst by now. Eventually it was six months before they were to have any news of our survival after being posted as "missing". Many of us including myself, were very critical of our Army commanders. We felt betrayed and completely alone. There were murmurings of unrest and we began to talk of a raid by the Long Range Desert Group who could liberate us without too much risk. At the time of course, they were unfortunately occupied with the defence of Egypt. This group was notorious among us and we were well acquainted with their daring sorties deep into enemy lines. Montgomery did not approve of the Long Range Group but others in authority looked upon them kindly and their work continued.

Summer passed into autumn which brought torrential rain to add to our discomfort. The camp turned into a soggy mess. We still wore our desert clothes and they failed to insulate us against the cold and the wet. We were a sorry bunch, forlornly clinging to the hope that the desert campaign must surely reach a climax soon, and with it would come our release. With this in mind we hung on to our sanity, but encouraging news of any kind was scarce.

Looking back, we were not so fortunate as those prisoners trapped in the hellholes of the Far East, suffering four years of the most sickening deprivation.

Many weeks later, when most of us had reached the farthermost limit of our endurance, a suggestion of excitement began to stir the prisoners, and little clutches of men could be seen talking in hushed voices in the camp. Then the good news streaked across the compound, like sunshine breaking out from beyond the clouds. The Eighth Army had smashed through the German line at Alamein and was racing westwards across the desert towards us with Rommel's Africa Corps in full retreat. We were jubilant, convinced that our captivity would end in just a few days. This was the moment we had all dreamed of during the past five weary months.

A few days later, we saw a convoy of trucks at the gate of the compound and our hearts sank. The Germans were not going to surrender us without a show and we saw our chance of freedom snatched from us. The British camp Commander was called to a meeting with the German command and he later told us that we were being evacuated to Italy where we would find better conditions in a permanent camp under the auspices of the Swiss Red Cross. We were promised new clothes and regular meals. Nobody could believe it. We were devastated.

Italy was a long distance from our present position. We estimated that the docks at Tripoli, our point of embarkation, were about four hundred miles away. The inevitability of the situation hung like a lead weight upon us, for we were in a position of such powerlessness. We were issued with one of the tasteless Italian biscuits and marched to the lorries. Two guards were at the tailboards and no time was wasted in beginning our journey. Some of the die-hards still talked of escape but most of us had abandoned all thoughts of getting away. We were no longer in any physical condition for daring escape attempts.

It was now mid-November, our sixth month on bread and water. We could no longer imagine eating a cooked meal, and the thought of tasting tea and coffee was very remote. We were tired and wasted, blanched with hunger and disappointment on our way to more unknown territory. The journey was arduous but during one of our toilet breaks, we conversed with one of the guards and he told us that the Eighth Army had passed Tobruk and were heading for Benghazi. We were being kept one jump ahead of them and could only hope for a miracle.

Towards evening after covering about two hundred miles, we approached an old fort which looked something out of "Beau Geste". It was an old cavalry barracks and we were herded into the stalls once occupied by the horses. The ground had been covered with straw to give a small amount of comfort, and a long gulley ran the length of the building which serves as a urinal for the prisoners, numbering some three hundred. It had obviously been used before our arrival and the smell was overpowering. There were a few latrines in the corners, flat sinks set into the ground with no running water. There was a ghastly mess with so many of the men suffering with dysentery. We settled down to sleep, trying to ignore the appalling stench and the general discomfort of the straw blankets. It was lucky that the Tarhuna cavalry barracks were just an overnight stop.

Next day, we passed through a number of Mussolini's desert settlements and were able to get fresh water supplies. These were bleak places and we could not understand why anyone would choose to live in them. Our journey continued throughout the day, and our next experience of overnight accommodation surpassed the previous one. We were placed in a tented compound containing the largest fleas any of us had ever seen. They swarmed over the camp in their millions, jumping on our legs as soon as we stepped foot in the place. Dismally, we tried to ignore the livestock. Diverting ourselves in trying to satisfy our craving for tobacco, which we found stronger as our hunger increased. We smoked dry cane, sucking up the smoke through the hollow stem, but it was so pungent that it burnt our lungs and we had to stop. Settling down to sleep attracted even more fleas and the misery of the night was spent twisting and scratching.

As if by surprise, our desert days came to an end when we reached the docks of Tripoli. Feelings were mixed and some of the men close to tears. As far as I was concerned, Europe was the point of no return and the prospect of years of confinement stretched before me. I left the desert with the feeling of sadness and affection. The past year had been such an overwhelming experience. The awesome vastness of the ancient sands had never ceased to fascinate me and we witnessed much of the reality of life and death in this great ocean of sand so far from our home and way of life. We had seen hunger, thirst, drama and comedy, tragedy, pain and fear, and not least of all of these, beauty; velvet night skies, jeweled and silent, the sands dotted with the wandering Bedouin. They were strange, drifting people, pursuing their way of life in the eye of the war whilst the gunfire and turmoil rages around them. They watched a demented civilisation pass through their lives and waited only to wander for another thousand years. I wondered how many of our landmines would remain hidden in the sand, making their journeys more perilous: the vicious instruments of war, a legacy from the educated and civilised men who had ravaged their land. And yet in springtime, parts of the desert became clothed in a mass of colour. Long grass and myriads of wild flowers blossomed in an otherwise arid landscape. As the desert hares leapt and bounded you could lay in the long grass, breathing in its fragrance and the war seemed very remote.

Specific landmarks were few and far between. We had to navigate by compass bearings. Certain vehicles carried a sun compass, near the driver. It resembled a miniature sundial, tilted at a given angle to suit that particular hemisphere and the falling shadow indicated the direction. One landmark we used near Gazala was an unexploded sixteen-inch naval shell, which had slithered across the desert. We could rely on it not being moved and always trod reverently around it when we visited the spot. It had a strange magnetism for us. We were attracted to it like moths round a flame and my back would tingle whenever I saw it. Our twenty-five pounders made a considerable explosion, but I could hardly imagine what this monster would be like.

Chapter Four

Transfer to Italy

At the docks in Tripoli, they wasted no time in herding us aboard ship. The vessel was loaded and ready to sail and we were packed tightly into a dark hold. After the brilliant sunshine, it took some time for our eyes to become accustomed to the gloom and when the last man was down, the entrance was partly closed, leaving an aperture of about four feet square. No one spoke and we sat on the floor which was slatted presumably to allow the sea water to pass through. Almost immediately, the engines began to throb and the ship got underway. I had thought of the bombers that we had seen daily heading towards these parts and prayed the intelligence services would know of these prison ships for if we were bombed or torpedoed there would be few survivors. As the day wore on, four men at a time were allowed out at a time to use the toilets built along the rail. It was such a long wait that a permanent queue formed at the bottom of the steps waiting to get out. Many of the prisoners with dysentery and other could not contain them selves in discomfort any longer began to urinate and vomit where they sat allowing it to pass through the slatted flooring. It was only when we heard the screams of anger coming up from the dark depths below that we realised there were more prisoners beneath us and the filth was dropping onto them. Until this moment there had been no indication of their presence. We had thought that our own conditions were bad but those poor devils below the waterline were even worse off and they would not be able to clean themselves until we reached Italy. Word spread quickly to use only the extreme far corners to urinate and it would run down the steel walls without fouling the people below. It was an awful business but there was no alternative at all. The discomfort of waiting was too much to bear. Sitting hour after hour in a dark hold with nothing to smoke, nothing to eat and only my faithful water bottle to support my flagging morale, I let my thoughts free of the stinking hold and thought back to lovely summer days in England.

Sitting on a steamer cruising down the Thames, we wore our Sunday best, sports coats flannels. Happy faces and pretty girls in summer dresses surrounded us. Music floated up from below as happy people danced. Here in the stench and the gloom, I wondered where it all went wrong. Later in the afternoon, I felt that I must get a glimpse of the world outside and got up to join the queue at the steps. It would be a long wait and as we inched our way along I resorted to my game of flashbacks to pass the time.

I recalled queuing at the local cinema, waiting for hours to see Fred Astaire and Ginger Rogers, shuffling along with a bag of peanuts and hoping to get in before the big film started. We would wait and wait, even if it meant standing around inside with a lovely usherette spraying disinfectant all over us with a huge pump.

This was a queue of a nightmarish kind, here in the hold of the prison ship. When I reached the top of the steps, I poked my head to be greeted by a German with a machine gun. He beckoned me forward and with three others I emerged into the bright sunshine feeling like the Count of Monte Cristo. We stumbled towards the latrines at the rail and were ordered to be quick. I drank in the scene in one great gulp. The blue sky, green sea, the seabirds wheeling and screeching, crowds of Germans on the deck and a machine gun pointing down from the bridge. The air was sweetly fragrant after the stink of urine and sweaty bodies. Leaving the toilet, we were quickly hustled back, not with force but quiet firmness. It was over too quickly, that brief glimpse, but at least I had escaped for a moment and the respite was a great help. After so many hours in the hold, all track of time was lost and we slept intermittently on the steel floor. Eventually the news raced round that we would shortly be arriving in Naples and we began to rouse ourselves. Surprisingly enough, there remained a vestige of humour in those rare characters who refused to be crushed under any circumstances, and we shared a laugh at their wit "See Naples and bleeding well die".

We arrived at the port of Naples and disembarked to assemble in well-guarded ranks on the quayside. Our own little group had managed to stay together and was among the first batch to march out into the streets of Naples. We were a forlorn lot, dirty and unshaven, thin and starved in our ragged desert clothing. Some had found the going tough and looked desperately ill. Ahead, we saw people lining both sides of the street and we tensed ourselves wearily for a hostile reception. To our surprise it was quite the reverse. The Italians watched our slow progress through the streets in an aura of sympathetic quietness. There was no animosity. The only sound came from our tired, marching feet and we sensed the goodwill of the onlookers as we neared the station. The prisoners walked with dignity, head held high, staring back into the eyes of the curious populace. Several women had tears in their eyes and many of the warmhearted Neopolitan mammas were sobbing, no doubt thinking of their own loved ones caught up in the carnage of an unwanted war. Many of them had gone to the frozen wastes of Russia, never to return. Several people came forward against the orders of the guards, handing bread and fruit to the prisoners, and some of the men were given cigarettes, I was hoping for a smoke but unfortunately never got near enough. This was genuine concern from the kindly Italians, and a gesture never to be forgotten. At that moment the war seemed to make no sense to me.

The prison camp at Capua was a reception centre and we were told that it would be a short stay before being transferred further north. The place was well organized in sharp contrast to the previous crude conditions in the desert and we received our first hot meal in six months. No words can describe that ambrosial macaroni stew, piping hot with meat and vegetables and a wedge of bread. We had long since forgotten the taste of cooked food, and like Oliver Twist, could have asked for much more, but were advised to be careful for a few days. In addition to this luxury, we were issued with British cigarettes, and replete, we sank down into our bunks, exhausted after our journey, too tired to wash and shave until the following day.

In the morning, we found that the camp had showers and toilets with running water and after a good clean up, representatives of the Swiss Red Cross took particulars of our capture, who informed us that our families would be notified as soon as possible that we were safe and well and prisoners of war in Italy. After being posted and "Missing in Action" for the past six months we could appreciate how worried they would be. True to their word, the Red Cross did notify them in a few days. The sick men were now able to receive treatment and were issued with a special medical parcel containing all kinds of nourishing foods to help build up their strength and the rest of us received the standard Red Cross issue; meat, butter, biscuits, tea, sugar and dried milk powder. At last we were able to enjoy a drink of warm tea, though from an empty meat tin, swimming in grease. Hot water was issued twice daily at the cookhouse for drinking purposes.

Some days later, we were moved to the station en route to a permanent camp. The majority of us were put into cattle trucks with wooden benches although many of the prisoners were in carriages and on the way north the train pulled into Rome station. It was early morning and the platforms were crowded with smartly dressed people on their way to work: sleek men, elegant women and dark beautiful girls. Our two worlds seemed poles apart. We looked out from our captivity at an ordinary workday, a world of freedom and city life. As they gazed curiously at us, the prisoners began to howl like animals putting on a show to protest about this mode of transportation and we mimicked farmyard noises. There was no animosity and everyone had a good laugh, even the guards. The girls were laughing at the antics of the sex-starved men who were whistling and waving to attract their attention. After so many months in the desert it was pleasant to see ordinary life again and remember that there was some other existence than this. It made me acutely aware of the value of all that I was denied as a prisoner and thoughts of escape began to emerge again now that I was feeling stronger.

Christmas was only a week away. Life for the unsuspecting Italians was continuing. How could they foresee the terrible bloodshed and destruction that was to ravage their beautiful land in the following year with the Allied landings and the ensuing battles of German resistance?

As the train lumbered through the countryside, it seemed that our wanderings would never end, and the prospect of finally ending up in Germany loomed closer with each passing hour. I was filled with a sense of foreboding, convinced that our fate would be sealed once we crossed the border. How would a defeated dictator behave towards his hostage prisoners? It was clear that we would be at the mercy of his volatile temper: a man whose dreams of conquest and domination would be thwarted. I feared the worst. The desire to break free grew as we travelled on. I had to get away before we reached Germany. Switzerland was the obvious choice, though it would mean internment for the duration of the war. The only alternative was through the south of France, then down through Spain and Gibraltar. That would mean a long journey through a Fascist country so I decided on Switzerland.

My plans had to be shelved, however, when we arrived in Liguria. We were shepherded from the train and marched along a country road towards our new camp. I tried to memorise details in the surrounding terrain. The ocean was a few miles to our left and the Apennine Mountains to our right. Through these landmarks, I was able to orientate myself somewhat. The most important detail to remain in my memory was that the doors of the villager's houses opened directly onto the road. This was to be a vital factor in my escape six months later.

The next camp was close to the road and contained three thousand men. It was the usual double barbed wire fence construction with a machine gun tower at each corner. The usual formalities of name, rank and number were gone through and a further search of our belongings. We were then allocated various huts and the prisoners we met there were most eager for any news of the war, naturally assuming that we had recently been captured. We could tell them nothing after our months in Benghazi and we were just as anxious to know what was happening as they were. I spoke to some of the men in the hut and found that they had been in captivity for two years. They seemed very depressed. A naval rating told me that he had been in the sea for twelve hours after his ship was bombed and had almost given up hope when he was rescued. Others had taken part in the bloody fighting when the Germans invaded Crete. They shared my views about being transported to Germany.

Our desert clothing was now in a poor state of repair and we were all feeling the cold. The Sergeant in charge noticed our condition and assured us that new uniforms would be provided. Sure enough, a few days later we were pleased to receive a complete change of clothes, including woollen underthings. It was good to feel clean again and indeed, that much warmer. We were also given an airmail letter and at last could write home to reassure our relatives after the long months of silence. I could imagine how worried my own parents would be.

Unfortunately, our clean condition was to be short-lived. Within a few weeks we became badly infested with lice. They crawled everywhere and we could do nothing to rid ourselves of them. I had seen the other men sitting around, picking over their clothes every day. I thought this only happened to other people. Now I was lousy too and did not scruple to join the daily ritual of searching the seams of my clothes, crushing the vermin between my thumbnails. All our blankets were infested and the lice-bitten nights were very unpleasant. In the Army, clothing and bedding could be fumigated but there were no such facilities in the prison camps and although we had a hot shower every two weeks it didn't seem to make much improvement. One day in the showers I saw lice crawling down the back of the man beside me, but by now I was immune to any sense of revulsion. We shaved all the hair from our bodies and although I had a very short hair cut, I could not bear to shave my head completely bald. The hairless prisoners looked so forlorn and I felt it must be the last straw to look as they did. I was determined to maintain some vestige of appearance. It was so painful when our body hair grew back again that I never bothered with shaving after that. Eventually I was lousy for nine months.

Our wooden bunks had slats across them to form a flat surface, and the previous occupant had used so many for brewing tea that the gaps between were now eighteen inches wide and the straw mattress kept sagging through. There was no way of replacing them, wood being in short supply for cooking and other more suspect purposes. Sometimes I found it more comfortable on the floor with the mice.

The problem of quickly boiling water for tea making had been solved with an ingenious device called a "blower". Constructed from old tins, which had been flattened and joined together they were fashioned into a stove with a belt-driven fan, and the result was something akin to a blacksmith's forge. They generated a tremendous amount of heat. Immediately after roll call, there was a stampede to the parade ground with everyone sitting like squaws, cranking like mad to produce the first brew. Some of the stoves were real works of art, so cleverly designed. Several months later and exhibition of handicrafts showed just how ingenious the prisoners were and I vividly recall a beautifully made coffee pot, complete with curved spout and domed lid, as lovely as if it had been professionally crafted. All this was achieved with improvised tools. Necessity had proved to be the mother of invention again, not only with these fine pieces of work but also with the secret tools of escape. I once heard of a pair of wire cutters being hardened with sugar acting a carbon to temper the soft steel.

Rather than spend my time fruitlessly resenting my incarceration, I forced myself to take an interest in the life of the camp. There was a multitude of talent and profession in the camp, and many volunteered providing interesting lectures on unusual subjects. I attended a number of talks from "Soil erosion in South Africa" to "Sheep shearing in New Zealand". Then there were the confessions of a Pullman Car attendant who worked on the railways of Britain. But strangely no one seemed to talk about survival or living off the land or problems related to escape. Everyone seemed to be wrapped in a world of make believe.

I had the desire to do something constructive and set about making a blower, removing two more slats from my bunk. This made the gaps even larger, of course, but I reasoned that the war might be over before I got any more clever ideas. Snapping off the rounded end of my smuggled knife gave a sharp corner to the metal, which enabled me to score a deep line on flattened tin cans and by bending the metal back and forth it broke off to form a perfectly straight line. Folding the edges together and beating them down with a stone made a fairly strong joint. I succeeded in making a workable piece of equipment, which would have won no prizes for elegance. It did sterling service at boiling water though.

There was a number of musicians in the camp who had somehow

obtained enough instruments to form a fine orchestra, and as the months passed, they daily rehearsed the score of the Mikado, which one genius had written from memory.

There were always plenty of mice in the hut, but they were not too much of a nuisance. On one occasion, however, they managed to spirit away my small piece of cheese, which I had try to preserve. Every week a piece of Parmesan cheese was issued to each hut and the sergeant in charge had the unenviable job of dissecting it into exactly equal parts with all eyes fastened limpet-like upon him. We usually found ourselves with a portion two inches long and one-inch square. I intended to keep mine for breakfast the next day and left it behind my bunk on a small shelf that I had rigged up. In the morning the whole piece had vanished, my ration for the week.

We got on fairly well with the Italian guards and whilst our one day on a working party, cleaning round the camp perimeter, our escort informed us that the war in North Africa was over and the invasion of Italy would not be long in coming. This was confirmed a few days later when we heard that there was a secret radio in the camp.

On a lovely, hot summers afternoon we were all laying outside basking in the sun when from over the camp loudspeaker system the sultry voice of a girl singing "Amapola" floated to us. Her slow, lilting voice drifted sensuously over the compound and the prisoners, in their enforced celibacy, sat up with interest. It did not take much imagination to picture her dark beauty. Someone remarked, "sex had reared its distant head". Over the next few weeks we had repeat performances and all agreed it was better than "Lily Marlene".

By midsummer the camp news bulletins seemed to be well organized with a small hand written sheet being passed from hut to hut. It was by this means that we heard the news of Sicily being invaded and the impression was given that a massive assault on the mainland could be launched at any moment.

Talking amongst ourselves, we all agreed that it would probably come to the north of us and sweep across to cut the country in half. From what we had seen of the terrain in the south, we thought it would be an impossible task to fight all the way up. For some reason, our daily bulletins suddenly ceased and the only news that we could get was from the guards. There seemed to be so many landings of the allied forces in the south that we were unable to form a true picture and rumours were running wild through the camp. Sometimes I think that the news was deliberately withheld from us and it was obvious that our liberation was not going to take place with an invasion in the north of the country. We could see our freedom gradually slipping away.

It was one day in September that we noticed with great excitement that our Italian guards had all disappeared. Even the machine gun towers were deserted but a few remaining soldiers shouted to us that the government had surrendered and Italy was out of the war. They laughingly declared that they were going home to their families. It was so sudden and unexpected that we were taken by surprise, unable to grasp what was really happening. We massed on the parade ground and the Regimental Sergeant Major in charge informed us we now came under the jurisdiction of the British Army and were to remain confined to the prison camp with the threat of court martial in anyone attempted to escape. The reason given for this perplexing order was that because the Allied Forces were rapidly advancing and would arrive in a few days, it would hamper their progress if we swarmed out all over the place. Eventually it took them eighteen months to get there. We lined up on parade to be lectured on military discipline by this misguided man and ordered to sing the national anthem while his cronies barred the way to the gate.

The prisoners were overjoyed at the thought of impending liberation and shook hands congratulating each other on our deliverance, exchanging addresses to keep in touch after the war. It was a scene of joy and relief but I sensed an uneasy feeling that it was all too easy. We had seen it all before in the desert, snatched away at the last moment when relief was so near, and I feared it could all happen again. I thought that we should get out quickly. Talking with the men, I suggested that we form a deputation to put our point of view to the camp commander, but we had all been so indoctrinated with army discipline over the years that there was no more enthusiasm for this sort of action, which may have been tantamount to mutiny. None would dare to question orders from an RSM. He was like God, seldom seen but his powerful presence was felt everywhere. As we deliberated, the Germans were racing down from the north to take over the camp and the precious time left to escape was running out like sand through an hourglass. The buzz of the excited prisoners faded into a deathly silence and we watched in shocked dismay as a column of lorries roared to a halt on the road above the camp and German soldiers were dismounting, racing towards us and encircling the camp.

For a moment, I froze in disbelief. My fears had been justified. They did not intend to lose us. I was not going to be thwarted now, and in an instant decided to make a break for it. I dashed to the rear of the camp with the intention of scaling the wire and leaping across the gap as far as possible, taking a chance on the mines. Several other men were beside me with the same wild idea. I clambered to the top of the fence, my heart pounding in trepidation on the point of making my jump for freedom. A line of German troops emerged from the woods beyond the cage, machine guns pointing towards us. Our move had been anticipated, and expecting a hail of bullets I was relieved when they motioned us to get down and back from the wire. I felt as though I had been crushed into the ground, so great was my disappointment. The golden opportunity had been lost and I felt a burning resentment towards the man who made the wrong decision and delivered us into the hands of the enemy. We could have scattered into the hills and take a chance of remaining free until the advance of the Allied Forces.

Chapter Five

My Bid for Freedom

After I had calmed down, I realised how extremely fortunate we had been in that the Germans had not fired on us during the frantic escape attempt over the wire. A wave of anger was sweeping the camp at those who had been responsible for our confinement and passions were roused to such an extent that I feared some action was going to be taken. The following day, however, these feelings seemed to be subdued when we heard with sinking hears the ominous news that I had been dreading. The camp was to be evacuated and all the prisoners transported to Germany.

The men were stunned. Many bowed their heads stifling the tears they longed to shed. How different from the elation of the previous day when we thought our captivity was to end. Wild ideas to find a hiding place within the compound were being considered in a desperate effort to remain behind and a few prisoners clambered up into the roof of the hut and the ceiling was nailed back behind them. Others burrowed into a huge pile of firewood behind the kitchen and even the latrines were explored for a possible place of concealment. I walked around the camp seeking a possible refuge but could find no suitable place. Now we had to try and gain our freedom the hard way. It was September 11th, 1943 and just nine months since our arrival. The next day, I was in the first batch of four hundred to line up on the parade ground for the grim trek to Germany. An office lectured us on the merits of good behaviour and said, "you will be well treated".

I thought about the danger we now faced: to be caged up in a country itself faced with humiliating defeat and destruction, unconditional surrender as the ultimatum. Our chances of survival would inevitably be slim. These thoughts ran through my mind as we waited for the gates to open, as in the days of our recreational walks, but this was to be a walk with a difference. Grim faced men plodding along silently with all the vestige of humour drained from their minds, filled with trepidation for what lay in store. We marched three abreast along that same narrow country road, which we had traversed from the station on our arrival in January. We were escorted by armed guards at four-yard intervals with an armoured car at the rear, its machine gun pointing along the column. It was some comfort to know that if I should manage to get away at least I had a little knowledge of the area. To be apprehended in the middle of an abortive escape attempt would earn me the reputation of being the escaping type. This would mean extra surveillance and further difficulties. It had to be one successful bid before reaching the station and being locked in a truck with no hope of release.

Over the past months there had been no chance to build up a stock of food as all Red Cross tins were being punctured before being issued to us to prevent hoarding for an escape. I had decided to live off the land if I could, existing on anything I could find. After marching for about four miles we were allowed to rest for a while. We sat on a narrow grass verge, and I found myself close to a thick hedge. The guards were smoking and chatting and a few trees on a slight bend obscured the armoured car. Trying not to attract attention, I thrust myself through the hedge making a whole large enough to squeeze my body through. Cautiously, I turned round and pushed my head through the gap and saw that there was a sheer drop of about twelve feet. The ground at the bottom was soft and cultivated, but there was a row of wooden poles with beans growing on them leaving a strip of about two feet wide from the wall. It meant dropping straight down the face in the hope that I would not suffer any injury.

My deliberations were suddenly interrupted with the guards approaching, ordering us to move on. Too late! I had hesitated and lost a good opportunity but it proved to be an object lesson for the future. Split second decisions had to be made and acted upon without wasting a moment. It was a hot afternoon and the march was log and exhausting.

We wore khaki uniforms and woollen underclothes that were soaked in perspiration. No one spoke and we all seemed to be resigned to our fate as each step took us to the station and Germany. The pace was slowing down and the straggling prisoners had to be urged on by the guards. As we plodded on, I saw the backs of several houses some two hundred yards away. I was about half way along the column and saw that the leading men at the head were disappearing from view round a sharp right hand bend in the road. In a flash I saw that this was the chance I had been waiting for. I remembered my observation of some months ago that the doors of the houses opened directly on to the road. Once round that corner I would be unobserved by the guard behind me for just a second or two. Looking behind I saw that he was ten feet away, and as our eyes met, he stared directly at me as though he knew what I was about to attempt. He would not see me from around the corner and the guard in front would have no reason to look back. Over to my left, they would be looking along the road, to their front to watch for the danger of oncoming traffic. All these things flashed through my mind at an incredible speed as the fateful bend approached. My heart was pounding and I began to tremble uncontrollably. Why risk it? It was foolhardy and impossible. Stay in line and be safe. Forget all about it! But I knew this was my last chance. I was almost there now and strangely, I felt calm as I tensed to my break. At last I rounded the corner and saw a door to my right. Dropping my haversack, I lunged forward and twisted the knob. Thanks God, it opened.

Stumbling through, I closed it behind me as the guard's heavy steps passed by. It had been split second timing. I had succeeded. Racing through the house, I came face to face with an elderly woman and as I fled past she raised her hands in terror thinking that I was about to attack her. I put my finger to my lips in a silent plea for her not to cry out, and ran through the kitchen to the garden beyond. I blundered through the hedge at the bottom and ran uphill for the shelter of the wood. I was in full view from the road and glancing back, I saw the whole column snaking its way along. Luck had been with me and my departure had not been noticed. Moving higher up into the trees I began to tremble again and my lungs burned. I was too exhausted to climb any higher and when

I reached some dense undergrowth, burrowed my way inside. It was cool and shaded, giving excellent cover under the ferns and bracken. I stripped to the waist and stretched out until my panting stopped and I calmed down.

Somewhere, a clock chimed four, and as I went through my pockets I weighed up my chances of remaining liberty until the arrival of the Allied forces presumably within a few days. I began to worry that the elderly lady in the house would inform the Carabiniere or the Germans of my whereabouts and start off a search, so I resolved to make a run for it again rather than be retaken at this stage. I still possessed a few cigarettes and matches and could not resist the urge to smoke as my mind raced over the events leading up to my escape. Unfortunately, my present position was on the wrong side of the road, and to make my way into the Apennines meant going back past the houses. It happened to be Sunday and folk would not be retiring very early. This meant it would be safer to wait to midnight before making a move. A terrible thirst was plaguing me.

Towards evening I heard the voices of a man and a woman calling softly. I did not understand the language at that time and I kept quiet, fearing a trap. They moved away and I relaxed again, biding my time. Just after midnight I set off. There was no moon but it was not completely dark. Like the nocturnal creatures, I was able to find my way without difficulty and quietly retraced my steps down to the houses. Climbing back into the gardens, I could see an alley between the buildings leading to the road and listened for a few minutes before darting across like a shadow to the other side only to be confronted by a thick hedge affording no passage through. Walking along for a few yards I panicked and returned to the alley to wait until I had calmed down. At last I felt able to set off again but at least it was fifty yards before I could force my way through.

I was in a cultivated area with all kinds of vegetables, and groping among some vines, found to my surprise and delight, great, plump bunches of grapes, luscious and ready for eating. It was exactly what was needed to quench my raging thirst and was indeed manna from heaven. In all the excitement of the last few days, it had not occurred to me that this was harvest time and in such an agricultural country there would be an abundance of food.

Continuing in the darkness, progress was difficult and could result in a twisted ankle so I settled down under a tree to wait for first light. It was a warm night and I listened to all of the sounds of the wild creatures and saw my first glowworms. After a few hours of intermittent sleep, I awoke with the sun streaming down on me and as I looked around it seemed to be like the very Garden of Eden. After the dry desert and the prison camps to be surrounded with lush fruit and green corn was an unexpected cornucopia. Not far away, I delivered a stone tank filled with cool, fresh water. How lucky could I be? A hundred yards in front I could see a river, which would have to be forded, and there was no sign of a bridge. I wanted to get away from the area and begin the uphill climb into the mountains before the local people began to appear. Stuffing my tunic with as many grapes, tomatoes and corn as I could carry, I made for the river. It appeared to be about two feet deep and twenty yards wide, and there was no option but to wade across. I wanted to keep my trousers dry and took them off and tied them around my neck. The water was icy cold but refreshing and afterwards I carried on with the intention of drying my legs before replacing my trousers.

Some time later, while following a narrow path in the hills, I rounded a bend and came upon a woman dressed in black, filling her jug at the spring. On hearing my approach, she turned, screamed in horror and dropped her jug. She fled in panic towards her house. I must have cut a strange figure in my underpants, tunic bulging with stolen vegetables and trousers round my neck. Her husband could appear with a shotgun, so I took a long drink and made a wide detour as quickly as possible. Later on I wondered how she would convince her family about the weird apparition she had seen. I did not want any more encounters of that nature so I later made the effort to improve my appearance and combed my hair down with a piece of gorse.

Two men working in a field wee gazing curiously at me, but they made no comment and as I left them behind I came to a wide main road with vehicles constantly passing. Many of them were military convoys and my route lay across into the trees beyond. There had to be a right moment to make the dash for cover, and it came at last. It was a hard climb up a steep face covered in undergrowth and loose boulders with no path to follow. I was glad to rest at the top and finish off my grapes. From the vantage point I looked back towards the prison camp and saw the blue Mediterranean beyond. Over to the left was a large coastal town covered in smoky haze. At least I was heading in the right direction. On reaching a thick wood I could hear the rumble of heavy gunfire coming from the south. This led me to believe that the front was about ten miles away and I panned to hide where I was until it advanced.

Casting about for somewhere to hide, I saw a tiny thatched barn, well hidden and half filled with dry leaves. It was the ideal shelter. Wrapping the remaining corn and grain in my tunic, and jamming up into the straw roof, I set off in search of water. Lack of food would not worry me but it was essential to have water. I emerged from the other side of the wood and drank in the glorious panorama of the Italian countryside. Miles to the south lay Tuscany and in the north I could see the snow capped Alps soaring majestically into the blue sky. Across the valley, chestnut trees covered the hillsides and small villages nestled peacefully in the gorgeous scenery. Far below, I heard the tinkle of a cowbell. A child was taking the animals to pasture. As I rested on the sun drenched hillside I thought of the countless thousands from all walks of life locked in a bloody combat far from their homes defending the precious freedom, which I had lost and so recently regained. I would know that I would go to extreme lengths to avoid recapture. War and danger seemed very distant from all the tranquility and I reflected on my present good fortune. It was my second day at large and the exhilaration of being at liberty after more than a year behind the barbed wire of prison camps could not be expressed in mere words. The scent of freedom was in the air and how fragrant it was! Until now the phrase "For King and Country" had been an abstract one, applied without meaning on recruiting posters and the roll of honour at my school which I saw every day as a child. "They died for King and Country". I think that it was here, at this place that I came of age and really appreciated what it was all about. The sacrifice that so many people had made through the centuries against those who sought to change our stable way of life.

As evening approached, I made my way down to the nearest houses and staying amongst the grapevines stay hidden. Some way from the buildings, I noticed another stone tank filled with water, and on the side was a large hollowed out gourd, obviously used as a scoop. There seemed to be no one about and after picking a few grapes and tomatoes, I filled the gourd and made my way back to the barn before dark. Now I had it all, food, water and shelter. I could sit back and await the Liberators. Before sleeping among the leaves I made a hole at the back of the barn and piled up brushwood and ferns. I was rapidly learning the ways of the wild creatures and could make a quick exit if danger threatened. Every evening I returned to the houses for food and water, taking care to get vegetables from different places each time, hoping to keep the borrowing in a low profile.

I was beginning to lose all track of time and it was only when the church bells rang that I knew it was Sunday again and just one week since I had escaped. The distant gunfire had died away and I was puzzled by the lack of military activity. I decided that after a few more days I would try and make my way to the front. My confidence was growing so that I did not wait until evening to go down to the houses, although I kept to my hidden paths. About the middle of the second week, after having a wash at the tank, I returned to sit on the side of the hill when I heard a plane approaching from the north. It was a small German reconnaissance aircraft and it passed over at about one thousand feet, circling the valley and returning much lower as though taking a closer look. I was still wearing my army uniform, but when it came back for a third time, I ran for the greater camouflage of the trees expecting a hail of bullets. But to my amazement, a massive shower of leaflets fluttered down from the plane. There were so many that I had only to reach out and pluck them from the air. The message was brief and to the point, in four languages. They advised escaped prisoners to give themselves up without punishment under an amnesty and anyone taking up arms would face the death penalty as a "Franc-Tyreur". I did not know what this was but could easily guess. Sniper or sharpshooter Any civilian aiding an escaper would face death as a traitor and a reward was offered for our recapture.

Stuffing a few leaflets in my pocket for future use, I returned to the barn. I did not take the threat lightly and remembered it many months later when I joined the partisans. Thinking over my next move, I knew that I would have to get civilian clothes somehow. My uniform was too conspicuous and although fair hair and blue eyes were not an asset in this country, at least I could make the effort to dress like a peasant. I looked around from above the valley community during the evening hoping to see washing hanging out to dry, but with no luck. A few days later I left my little barn refuge to walk south. The going was hot and arduous, making my way across the hills, keeping clear of recognised paths, making detours to avoid small villages. After several hours, I had not made any appreciable progress and during the late afternoon, I came to the outskirts of an isolated community. There was a small schoolhouse, and peering through a side window the children's desks were visible and I noticed drawings pinned to the walls. Hoping to find something useful in the way of food and clothing, I climbed through an unlatched window. A vase of flowers stood on the teacher's desk and I drank the water gratefully. Opening one of the cupboards, I found only books and papers, but on the wall, to my delight was a small map of Italy that I removed from its frame. It was most useful and I was able to pinpoint my position.

I sat at one of the little desks, looking at the blackboard and pictures around the walls. The years rolled away to my own schooldays of 1926 with the impeccably dressed teachers in smart suits, white shirts and cufflinks. They commanded the greatest respect from us all. Their word was the law and we believed everything that we were told without question. They were all serious men, devoid of any humour, for most of them had endured the horrors of the First World War in France and would never talk of their experiences even though we longed to hear their tales of glory. One master had a piece of shrapnel in his wrist, which he would twiddle during his lectures and we understood that our headmaster, whose face was badly scarred, had been decorated for gallantry.

While we scribbled, the teacher would move quietly around the class peering down from behind at all our efforts. The teachers' clothes smelled heavily of pipe tobacco, which added to their aura of well-dressed authority. I could always sense the teacher's presence behind me, though he made no sound and my back would tingle waiting for his fury to erupt at my poor efforts. Without moving my head I could see him glide past to hover behind the next trembling boy. They used the cane freely on palms and bottoms over the most paltry misdemeanours, and at our tender age it really hurt. Woe betide the boy who showed any emotion afterwards: his reputation would be lost forever with his classmates. We had to return to our desks with a sickly smile of pain on our faces until the sting passed, basking in the admiring glances of the others for the rest of the lesson. The harder the caning, the greater was the admiration for the victim.

Towards dusk, I left the schoolhouse, again using the window, intending to find somewhere to settle down for the night. Not far way, I came upon the village cemetery. The iron gates were unlocked and at the rear I found a secluded spot to lay down until dawn when I planned to look for something to eat. I decided to use the mountain paths as much as possible. It would be too long and difficult a journey to go across country. Making myself comfortable in the grass behind the tombs, I listened to the sounds of the night, feeling relaxed and secure. Nothing mattered now but to remain at large. Physical discomforts were secondary to the joy of being free and I wondered, with a feeling of cautious excitement what I would encounter the next day. The following morning I studied my map and saw that I would have to travel in a south-easterly direction. Keeping to a track down through the valley was easier than going across country and at the bottom I found a fast flowing river, enabling me to have a wash and a drink. I felt refreshed and followed the path to the next wooded hill. Some time later a group of people appeared coming towards me, and I waited in the undergrowth for them to pass. There were several young men and women laughing and singing, all carrying baskets. They looked so happy, anything but hostile, almost tempting me to call out. Obviously they would have food and wine with them but caution was uppermost in my mind and I let them pass before moving on.

By late afternoon I had made good progress and could see a small church nesting quietly in the distant hills. I was feeling tired and hungry, what better place for to seek refuge than the House of God. I thought of the stories I had read, of those in dire straits finding sanctuary. The church seemed quite deserted but the door was unlocked and inside the atmosphere was cool and tranquil. I sat in a far corner and took the serene beauty of the altar. A light tang on incense added to the sacred mystique and I felt calm and relaxed, thinking of my young days at Sunday church all scrubbed and polished in respect for the Sabbath.

After a short rest, I made my way to the side of the building and saw a flight of steps, presumably leading to the priest's quarters. I called out and received no reply so ascended the stairs and found myself in a sparsely furnished room with bare boards. A dining table and chairs stood in the centre and a carved bench along one wall. I shouted again but there was still no response and not wishing to intrude further, I left and went outside. I tried another door and discovered a kitchen with a bucket of water and a ladle on a chair. Whilst enjoying a cool drink there came a patter of wooden shoes and a woman appeared in the doorway. She was startled by the unexpected confrontation and I was relieved when she did not scream. Pointing to the water, I indicated that I wanted a drink and she nodded. She had recovered her composure by now and seeing my uniform asked if I was a German. With my limited Italian, I was able to convey to her that I was a British soldier making my way to the south. Showing her my prison camp lira, she was convinced. Her face lit up with a smile as she relaxed her defensive stance. Pointing to her wedding ring she said that her husband was missing in Russia, along with many others from the locality. Her eyes were moist as she spoke of him, condemning the war and all the misery it had brought to so many ordinary people. Nodding towards the table she motioned me to sit down while she prepared a meal of bread and cheese with a cup of milk. Never had food tasted so good after two weeks on fruit and vegetables and I thanks her warmly for her kind gesture.

Afterwards she indicated with the peculiar, idiosyncratic Italian wave of the hand that I was to follow her up to the living room where I had been previously, and I was introduced to the priest who shook my hand and made me welcome. He was an elderly man with a short grey beard and a solemn countenance. He was able to speak a little English and using a strange mixture of German and Italian, we made ourselves understood. He said that the housekeeper, Maria, would later cook a meal for us and that I was welcome to stay. On learning that my home was in London he asked about the bombing and if there had been much damage, shaking his head sadly. He asked about St Paul's Cathedral and said that many beautiful places would be lost if the war carried on. A few months later I thought of him when the ancient monastery at Cassino was devastated in the allied advance after standing for a thousand years. The Germans made great propaganda out of the wave of anger that subsequently ran through the country.

In the evening, Maria brought us an enjoyable meal. The priest apologised for its shortcomings due to rationing, but I thought it delicious. We talked over coffee later on and he reminded me that the following day was Sunday and that many people would be coming to church. I had now been free for two weeks and we agreed I should stay hidden until after the service. He made no comment when I said that I was not a Catholic and I did not attempt to discuss religion. He asked if I was tired and called Maria to show me to a bedroom, bidding me goodnight and saying that he would pray for my safe return home. After thanking him for his hospitality, the housekeeper took me to a small candlelit room with a single bed in it and sacred pictures upon the walls. When she had gone I looked at the beautifully carved walnut bed with snowy white sheets and lacy pillow perfumed with lavender and felt I could not soil it with my unclean condition. Still infested with lice, it would have been such an abuse of their kindness, almost sacrilege. It was a long time since I had seen such a bed and so I convinced myself that I would sleep more comfortably on the floor. My tunic served as a pillow and I reclined on a rug at the side of the room with ictuses of angels and the Virgin Mary smiling down at me as though amused at my scruples.

I began to feel some remorse at my lack of faith and pondered if it could have been something other than just luck, which had seen me through the past three years. The priest's kindness had to be a true expression of Christian principles and I realised that the devout always had something to turn to for comfort in times of stress. Disbelievers had no shield at all against life's pain and anguish. I fell asleep with a picture of the Good Samaritan in my mind and although I was tired, it was an uneasy sleep. I awoke soon afterwards imagining I could hear heavy footsteps outside the window. Being confined between four walls and made me feel insecure and it was early morning before I really slept. I came to consciousness hours later, bathed in warm sunshine to the sound of sacred hymns with the Madonna and the Angels looking down at me. I thought I had died in the night and passed away. It made me sad and I wondered how my family would take it.

The housekeeper's face appeared and her voice brought me back to reality, as though falling from a great height. She asked why I had not slept in bed and I avoided the real reason saying it was too soft and I preferred the floor. She accepted my explanation and left, returning later with a breakfast of bread and milk. Looking from the window she called me over to see the congregation leaving the church and gathering on the terrace outside, all smartly dressed, the women in black clutching their bibles and silk headscarves. People would be coming and going all day and she thought it best that I stay in the room until evening when I could share a meal with the priest.

During the afternoon, I heard the sound of music and looking down through the trees I could see a group of young people dancing a mazourka to the strains of a portable gramophone. It was a happy scene, far removed from war and brutality. The day passed quickly and I felt refreshed. After an evening meal with the priest I showed him one of the pamphlets that the Germans had dropped. He dismissed it with a wave of the hand as though it was of no importance but he warned me of being careful. Many towns were Fascist and they would not all be friendly. When I was ready to leave the following day, Maria packed some food for me to take. I found it hard to resist their invitation to stay and as I thanked them, her eyes were moist with tears. She took my hand, wishing me good luck. Miles later, I felt lonely and empty. I turned and looked back across the hills to the church growing fainter in the distance with the certainty that I would never forget them.

I tried to avoid populated areas and had to make several detours that added distance to the journey and made it difficult to keep to the southeast. In the late evening with the darkness coming on, I had been unable to find shelter and settled down in the undergrowth opening a parcel of food that Maria had given me. It was bread, cheese and salame, with a piece of polenta made with maize. This was a very welcome meal indeed.

Although October was approaching the days were warm and sunny and the following afternoon I came upon a small community of about fifteen houses. Rather than make another tedious detour I decided to go straight through, keeping to a well-used path. This led me to a flight of steps by the side of a large house and I descended, passing a window, I heard the homely sound of crockery rattling. As I peered down I saw an elderly woman preparing a meal. Not wanting to cause alarm, I left quickly and walked through a terraced garden leading to a wood. It was secluded with a small stream. As I sat on the bank, feet in the water, pondering my next move I saw a girl coming through the trees from the direction of the house. There was no time to hide and keeping still, I hoped that she would pass without observing me, but she glanced over and stopped, frightened and suspicious. To allay her fears I called out and waved. She came slowly towards me, asking who I was and there was no alternative but hope that she would be friendly.

Conversation was difficult but I managed to make her understand that I had escaped from the Germans and was a British soldier. Her eyes widened in surprise asking where the prison camp had been. When I mentioned the name of the place she replied that she knew it quite well. She pointed up to the large house and said that it belonged to her father and that I should follow her. As we went up the steps, she told me that her name was Tina and I kept to my army name of Eddie.

At the rear of the house we went to a terrace garden and sat at a large wooden table. Tina said that she would bring something to eat. Looking out across the hills and valleys to the blue sea far in the distance, thoughts of danger and betrayal began to recede and I felt strangely at ease. As I relaxed I heard the sound of Tina's wooden shoes on the steps. I saw that an elderly woman who was carrying a tray accompanied her. She had bread with a bowl of soup on it. She smiled in a friendly way, inviting me to eat. During the meal they discussed the situation in their local dialect, which was impossible for me to follow, then Tina informed me that one of her neighbours had lived in America for many years and could speak English. As she left to find him, it occurred to me with some dismay that she might return with the Military Police. I watched the path preparing to take flight if my suspicions were confirmed and was relieved some time later when she came back with an elderly man wearing a cap.

Tina introduced him as "Luigi" and I took an instant liking to him. With his wrinkled face and twinkling eyes he laughed as we shook hands, asking in a deep Californian drawl: "Where in the hell" I had come from? I told him I would like to rest for a while continuing my journey south and he stared at me aghast saying I would never make it. The front was more than two hundred miles away and that they were fighting at Salerno. This was a disaster and I told him of the heavy gunfire I had heard previously leading me to think that the front was very close. He replied that it was "them goddam sons of bitches practicing". The German were building a defence line across Italy using forced labour. I knew that I had not the stamina to walk two hundred miles across country. I had counted on twenty at the most. Seeing my dismay, Luigi told me not to worry. "We'll look after you until they get here". We were not to know that there would be eighteen months of bitter fighting before the allied forces advanced that far. The Germans were poring in their best divisions to hold out and every mountain was fiercely contested with terrible losses to the advancing liberators against the enemy's most experienced fighters. All this raged while at home the comments of a certain lady member of parliament goaded many to bitterness. It was said in the House that the troops in Italy were having a fine time, drinking and lounging in the sun. The Eighth Army expressed their disgust in a ribald song to the tune of "Lili Marlene" condemning her remarks.

Luigi invited me to his home for a wash and a shave and here I met several of his neighbours who all seemed very friendly. He translated my remarks for their benefit. It was agreed that I should stay out of sight away from the houses in the woods above the village. With the Germans and Fascist militia rounding up men for forced labour and military service we would have to be careful. I showed him one of my pamphlets and he said that they had already seen them. Bringing out a newspaper he pointed to an article that offered substantial rewards for the recapture of escaped prisoners and it seemed as though others had escaped in the area. There was also a dire warning about aiding men on the run.

In the evening, Tina with Luigi and together we set out to find a suitable hiding place. On the way, we stopped at Tina's house where I met her mother, Rosa and her father, Pino. Rosa was a small dark-haired lady with brown eyes and a charming smile that put me at ease straight away. Pino was tall and slim, wearing a trilby and smoking a cigar. He poured me a glass of wine. It was through Luigi that I asked if they could let me have some civilian clothes. My uniform being conspicuous enough to arouse curiosity if any outsiders saw me in the vicinity. Pino said that he would bring some the following day. After thanking him and Rosa, we made our way up to a small barn well hidden and filled with dry leaves such as I had slept in the previous week. From this point I could see down into the village and as I settled down for the night I thought of the poor men who had been transported to Germany and I could see their unhappy faces. It had not been possible to share my plan with others but consoled myself with the thought that it must have encouraged some to take a similar attempt before it was too late. After three weeks I was still at large and how good it felt, in spite of the uncertainties of the future.

When Pino arrived with Luigi the following day he brought a complete change of clothing for me along with a blanket. I told Luigi that I was lousy and he chuckled. I would have to have a good scrub in the river before wearing any clean clothes. The water was cold at the bottom of the valley and after scouring myself with handfuls of leaves, I buried my khaki under the sand and stones. At last I felt clean and the civilian clothes were like silk after the heavy uniform. When Tina and Luigi came up later with a meal they had a good laugh at my appearance and called me "Contadino".

A few days later I met Tuglio. He was a young lad of about nineteen and very keen to learn English. Like so many of his friends, he wanted to go to America after the war hoping for a better life. In return for my coaching in English he helped me with Italian and came as often as possible, sharing his cigarettes. The Italian language had long intrigued me and as we struggled to teach each other I saw how beautiful he was.

As the weeks passed I began to put on weight and feel stronger. Occasionally Rosa would prepare a bath for me and would also bring a change of underclothes. I insisted that she maintain a sharp lookout from the window along the path leading to the road but she always waved my fears aside. To be caught would have meant a return to prison for me but the thought that I could bring harm to these kindly mountain people plagued me constantly and I was determined to observe the utmost caution in spite of their assurances that it was safe. One day, Rosa confided that she had a son about the same age as myself and when the war clouds had begun to gather, they had sent him to live with a uncle in California. She found comfort in the knowledge that he was far removed from danger and smiled happily as she spoke of him. Poor Rosa, how tragically wrong she was to be. Fate would deal them a terrible blow.

I began to go for long walks through the mountains, sometimes staying away for a few days and wherever I went I found hospitality at isolated farms, never mentioning my hideout at Zerna. Tuglio could see that I was feeling restless and invited me to work on the land with him. I badly needed the exercise and enjoyed the physical exertion. He had recently adopted a small brown terrier names 'Bobbie'. The little dog would sit and watch our every move as we worked. He seemed to share his affection equally between us and I made a great fuss of him. Looking down from my hideout one day, I saw him making his way through the village and I whistled through my fingers. He stopped and turned and as I whistled again, he came racing up through the trees, tail wagging, so pleased to find me. After that he came every day and we walked for miles together through the hills.

Weeks later, his visits suddenly ceased and I thought that he had tired of my company. But just after dawn one day, I heard the sound of rustling in the undergrowth. Someone was approaching without giving the recognition whistle that Tina and I had agreed upon, and I prepared to get out through the back of the barn. It was then that I heard a whimper and a small brown face appeared at the opening. Bobbie had returned but something was wrong. As he wriggled towards me through the leaves I was horrified to see that his little back was red raw. He had obviously been badly scalded. It must have happened many days previously and the skin was showing some signs of healing. As I cradled him in my arms he sighed and licked my hand. He stayed the next day wrapped in my blanket. Fortunately, he made a complete recovery.

Through Tina's good offices I met all the people of Zerna and worked with them hoping to earn my keep, but we had to be vigilant. With the increasing risk of early morning raids by the Germans, many of the young men were sleeping away from their homes in the woods and barns.

On one occasion, we had an amusing time when Tina and her friend tried to give me a haircut. It all ended in laughter and my hair in a terrible mess. They promised to ask the village barber to put it right and it was through this unfortunate topiary that I met Tony. He was badly disabled, having been born without legs. To move around he would swing his body up vertically and walk on his hands. As he trimmed my hair, he laughed and joked and in all the months that I knew him I never once saw him downhearted, facing life with a courage and fortitude that was an inspiration to all. He was always ready to greet you with a warm, cheerful smile in spite of his disability. I used to watch him slicing long branches into strips and patiently weaving them into beautiful baskets, chattering all the time as he worked. Whenever there was a social function of any sort he was never left out and his many friends would carry him, sometimes in one of his own baskets laughing all the way. I greatly admired him and he always made me welcome in his parent's home.

As winter drew on, Pino allowed me to sleep in an outhouse away from the main dwelling. It was the storeroom and wine cellar with bunches of grapes and preserved meat hanging on the beams. It was whilst sheltering here that I was able to watch Pino distilling "Grappa". This was a home-brewed alcohol made from old grapes and stewed in a large copper vat. It bubbled over a low fire, the steam condensed in a long tube and dropped slowly into a bottle. It was pure alcohol and quite illegal. The Fascists came down quite heavily on those unlucky enough to be caught, but it got a good price on the black market and many of the mountain people were willing to take the risk to supplement their meager income. Most of it eventually found its way to the city bars. I remember Pino sampling his brew with a roguish grin on his otherwise serious face, pronouncing it to be "WHISKEY". As contraband it was, no doubt, more flavoursome and as he tossed some into the fire, it exploded like petrol. This was my first introduction to it and during the afternoon he was busy elsewhere, I kept the fire tended in his absence, sampling a little at intervals to monitor its progress.

When Pino returned some hours later, the effects of the Grappa, combined with the heat from the fire had worked a marvelous change to me. I lurched unsteadily from the outhouse and when he heard my slurred speech he suspected what had been happening. With a grin, he advised me to stay outside for a while. It was several hours before my head cleared and realised that if there had been an emergency, I would have been too disorientated to think clearly.

One day, Pino had shown me a newspaper featuring a group photograph after they had been shot down. Their faces had all been retouched in the picture to give them an appearance of evil, their mouths twisted and their eyes distorted. They looked like grotesque monsters, so much so that it was amusing rather than frightening and the caption read "These are the faces of the gangsters who have come to bomb our cities". Pino told me that with many of his neighbours he had been a soldier in the First World War on the side of the Allies fighting the Austrians and commented on the futility of it all.

Although the outhouse or "Cantina", was warm and dry I found that it was difficult to sleep and the slightest sound woke me with an uneasy feeling. I often went out during the early hours and walked around the commune, sometimes seeing a local man, Mario, making his way to work in a copper mine across the valley. He carried a flickering acetylene lamp. At one time he passed within a few feet but I remained silent in order not to frighten him.

Whilst working with a family for a few days, I made the acquaintance of Aldo, a stocky dark man who wore a beret. I was pleased to discover that he could speak English. Like myself, he was on the run and was staying with his relatives at the home. A dedicated communist who had fought in the Spanish Civil War, he was wanted by the police and had fled from the city. He kept up a steady diatribe against the Fascists and their German allies. I invited him to accompany me to the south in an attempt to cross the line but he pointed out the difficulties and said that he was in touch with a resistance movement being formed in the north and he intended to join them. A few weeks later as he was leaving, we shook hands and he promised to return when he had more information about the movement, but the months passed and I never saw him again.

Throughout the winter, I longed for the spring to come and when at last the countryside blossomed in all its fragrant beauty, I was homesick for England and felt an overwhelming desire to move on to the south. When I told Tina and her mother my intention, Rosa wagged a stern finger at me and talked me out of it. Tina said that it would be more sensible to wait and see what was going to happen, and although I protested, they had their way and I postponed my departure.

A bitter struggle was taking place and the Germans were sending their best troops to halt the allied advance to Rome. It seemed to me that the liberation of the north was going to be a long fight over difficult country that favoured the defenders. Every mountain pass would be fiercely contested.

During one of the local religious festivals, there was a family gathering at Tina's house and many relatives from the city were there. I was invited to join them for dinner and they received me cordially, but when Rosa's brother in law arrived he made it clear that he resented my presence. A few days previously the American Air Force had bombed a railway bridge spanning the hills just a few miles away and many civilians living in the area had been killed. It had been a terrible tragedy for the mountain people and I could not understand his bitterness over the way in which the raid had been carried out. Although he was speaking in the local dialect I could make out enough of his speech to feel uncomfortable and I acted as though I had not understood what all the fuss was about. Rosa looked embarrassed and Pino stared at his plate. Tina pointed out that I was not to blame but he remained very belligerent. I felt I should leave but realised that Rosa would be very upset and although he calmed down during the meal, I tactfully took my leave afterwards when it was not obvious.

A few days later I encountered Tuglio going to work on the land for one of his neighbours and I jumped at his invitation to go with him. I needed something to do and people to talk to. Fumbling in his pocket with a triumphant grin he produced a piece of cigar that he crumbled in his hands and shared with me. We both rolled a cigarette and as we sat savouring every moment of the smoke, not knowing when we would get another, I helped him to struggle with his English. Eventually the talk turned to religion and I was surprised when he confessed that he was an agnostic, attending Mass only to please his family. Like me, he found it all confusing.

We made our way to a small cottage and were greeted by a woman and two little girls. Tuglio introduced me, calling her Signora Paula. She was a woman in her late twenties with black hair and dark, laughing eyes. She was almost gypsy-like in her appearance and wore a permanent good-natured smile. Later in the day, as we toiled in the land, she recounted the same tragic story that I had heard from the priest's housekeeper. For a while she became very serious and anxious as she spoke of her husband, a prisoner of war in Russia. I tried to reassure her that he would be well treated but she was clearly upset. Paula was very strong and worked as hard as any man to maintain some sort of life for herself and her small daughter. The two little girls were evacuees from the city and helped out with some of the easier jobs. With all the mountain people, life was one long round of hard work from dawn to dusk to ensure a good harvest from the terraces carved out of the hillside. Somehow the community managed to be almost self-supporting but with so many men absent the extra burden fell on the women and children. Everyone had a part to play and most families had a few livestock. The sheep provided wool, which the old ladies spun by hand, twirling a bobbin for hours on end. They would draw the fibres from a hank of wool held in a cleft stick.

While working far down at the bottom of the terraces with Paula and the little girls, we collected two massive bundles of firewood to take back to the home. Paula swung one of them up onto her back effortlessly, asking me to follow with the other. The two girls were watching as I tried to lift it up and anxious to show my strength., I fought to get underneath it, tottering about and almost falling over. They laughed and applauded my efforts as I began the long climb up a long flight of narrow steps. Somehow, I reached the top and lurched towards the house, swaying like a drunken man with my legs buckling under the weight. Paula was at the kitchen door, laughing and urging me on. If she felt and sympathy she didn't show it as I collapsed, panting for breath and soaked in perspiration. "Bravo" she said.

I helped the little girls light the kitchen fire and like many other cottages, the cooking arrangements were primitive, just a raised hearth in the middle of the floor and an iron pot hanging from a chain. For baking, an earthenware dish was heated in the flames and then covered with hot embers. It was very effective and bread baked this way was delicious. All the smoke and fumes went up through the slatted ceiling, drying out the autumn chestnut harvest to be ground into flour lately.

Paula showed me to the living room and then left to prepare a meal. Looking round the sparsely furnished room, with bare boards, I realised how terribly poor they were. There were no luxuries of any description and even the water had to be carried from a spring near the house. Glancing into an adjoining room I saw a dark blue suit next to a photograph of a sailing man in a military uniform. At that moment, Paula suddenly returned and as she looked at the picture of her husband, the bright smile melted away in a flood of tears. For a moment, I could see the heartache and the anguish that she tried so hard to conceal. She turned away, trying to hide her emotion, and looked from the window to the distant hills. In a low voice, she said that he would need the clothes when he returned. I said nothing to increase her suffering and tried to offer some words of comfort, although I feared for his safety at the hand of the Russians. Two years after the war had ended I returned to Zerna and sadly there had been no news on him. Over the next few weeks, I worked occasionally with Paula and the children, doing odd jobs and sleeping in a hayloft above the cowshed.

It was some distance from the house and during the early hours of one morning that I was alarmed by the sound of heavy feet running past the shed and pounding up the steps to the house, followed by a furious hammering on the door and someone shouting. Being fully dressed, even to wearing my boots, I made a quick getaway through the straw wall at the back of the loft and jumped down to the terrace below. I moved quickly through the darkness and slipped past the house into the woods, the banging on the door causing me to fear the worst. I kept away from the village the following day, returning after dark late at night. I approached the house stealthily. There was no sound, and after waiting for some time concealed in the undergrowth, I tossed a small pebble up on to the roof. As it rolled down the tiles, it's clatter seemed to be amplified in the silence, until I thought that the whole commune would be awakened. I heard the door being unbolted and Paula came down to the terrace calling my name in a soft voice. She explained that the commotion had been due to her brother's wife being taken ill and in a panic he had run to her for help. Although we laughed at what happened, the thought of what might have been only served to increase my determination not to become complacent about taking chances. This was brought home to me again a few days later when I saw Luigi. He called me over to his house to show the local newspaper. As he pointed to the front page I recognised the familiar face of a young South African by the name of Dinwoodie, who had been our camp postman. He had been recaptured in a sudden raid on an isolated village just a few miles away. The family who had sheltered him after his escape had all been arrested and only the fact that the daughter of the house was pregnant saved her life, although she was sent to prison. The local police chief was a vicious man working with the Gestapo and would stop at nothing to assert his brutal authority. After the war he received just punishment for the lives that he had taken.

It was a lovely Sunday afternoon towards the end of May when I met Ezzio. Tuglio and I had to join a game of football with a group of village boys behind the church on the only piece of flat ground in the commune. Looking towards the houses, I saw a young man on a tricycle making his way slowly, and with some difficulty along the uneven track behind us. He sat watching, enjoying our game and urging us on. After a while, Tuglio joined him and then waved me over to introduce him as Ezzio. He said that he had recently arrived from the city to stay at Zerna until the war was over. I noticed that he was severely disabled with both legs encased in steel calipers and his body was badly distorted. He greeted me warmly and I found that, as with Tony, his disability did not affect is sense of humour. He wanted to know all the details of my capture and subsequent escape from the Germans, laughing and joking as I recalled life behind the wire at the prison camp. His parents owned a bar in the city and we agreed to meet there after the war. When I did in fact return to Italy we had that drink together and spoke of our time at Zerna.

Until the outbreak of war he had made the yearly pilgrimage to Lourdes, stating quite confidently that one day he would be fit and well. So strong was this conviction that he had no doubts at all about an eventual cure. Inviting me to his home, he lowered his voice and said that he had brought a radio with him and I would be able to listen to news of the war from the Voice of London. We made our way back and he informed me that the prison camp was filled with Jewish civilians, taken from their homes awaiting deportation to Germany. For several nights we crowded round the radio, Tuglio and Tina explaining the news in a way which I could understand, and at last I was able to form a picture of what was happening. After the bulletins, we listened to coded messages from the resistance.

When passing Ezzio's house one morning in early June, he yelled excitedly to me from a window. As I walked towards him he shouted that the Allies had landed in Normandy. The room quickly filled with his neighbours and we listened in fascinated silence as the news unfolded. I was now confident that Hitler would withdraw his troops from Italy but the following months proved me wrong and they fought with even greater determination. It was going to be a long struggle.

Whilst working on one of the terraces a few weeks later, I saw Tina hurrying towards me, breathless and agitated. A stranger had arrived and was claiming to be English. He was at Luigi's house and they were worried that he may not be all that he claimed. I followed Tina to his hiding place and sat listening to their conversation without identifying myself to him and after some time I was convinced that he was genuine. There was no option than to accept his story and when at last I revealed to him that I too was on the run, he laughed at the circumstances under which we had met. As we shook hands, he introduced himself as Bill Kendall, a petty officer in the Royal Navy and I soon discovered that he spoke good Italian. I suggested that we make forces and make our way south, but he had already made his plans to go through the South of France, then down through Spain to Gibraltar. It was going to be a long walk but he was determined to try and the following day, as he departed, we all wished him luck. Watching his lonely progress across the hills to the north, I reflected on his courage and over the years I have often wondered if he was successful in his bid for freedom. When the news came that the Allies had captured Rome, although suffering terrible losses, I decided that I would follow Bill's example and make my way to the front.

Sitting on a grassy bank one day with Tuglio in the scorching heat, we discussed life in the mountains. Suddenly our conversation was curtailed by the appearance of two girls walking along the path below us. They were smartly dressed, looking quite of place in the countryside. Tuglio was acquainted with them and called a greeting. I watched them approach, thinking it safer not to disclose my identity. Both girls were very beautiful and Tuglio introduced them as "Anna and Maria". Anna was very fair, looking cool and lovely in a loose green and white dress. In sharp contrast Maria, raven-haired with dark eyes in a low-cut dress of bright red which clung tightly to her shapely figure. She joked with Tuglio in a low musical voice. After the sweat and tears of the past two years, during which time I had been very remote from female company, they were absolute visions of loveliness, and their presence was captivating. When they became curious about my continued silence, Tuglio revealed that I was a British soldier and it took them quite by surprise. Maria had suspected I was a German deserter.

On learning that I had escaped from the marching column, they said that they had seen my fellow prisoners being taken into the railway yard, under close guard and were intrigued to know how I had got away. As we chatted in the warm sun, their fragrant perfume floated around us in the afternoon air, heady and tantalising. Tuglio gave me a rascally grin, taking a long deep breath. He seemed to have a liking for city girls. My thoughts flashed back to those warm pre-war summer nights, dancing with pretty girls and remembering the sweet scent of "Soir de Paris" which would linger about our clothes for days afterwards: waiting for the last waltz to charge across the floor and sweep up the girls of our dreams. Then the long walk home and a midnight kiss on her doorstep. Now it all seemed like a hundred years ago.

When at last the girls had to return to their home, the encounter had passed all too quickly, and like Tuglio, I had enjoyed every moment of their vivacious company. As a parting gesture, they both wished me good luck, and as we watched them walk away, I commented on their appearance. Tuglio chuckled, giving me a knowing wink. He then disillusioned me by revealing they worked in the casino. Casino girls or not, they had been charming and friendly towards me but I could only hope that they would be discreet about my presence at Zerna. Although the mountain villages were isolated, news seemed to travel swiftly and I often heard items of gossip concerning places many miles away.

I had been curious about the partisan movement for many months and at this time, heard that there was some activity in a place to the south of us. From the information that I was able to gather, it seemed as though the country people were caught between two evils; the requests for food and sometimes shelter from the "rebels" (as the Germans called them), and on the other hand, the threat of execution and the destruction of their homes should they be caught. With the Allies advancing, the Fascists were ruthless in their treatment of anyone suspected of assisting the enemy. We had our first indication of partisan activity one night when a tremendous explosion thundered across the hills as they demolished a bridge.

A few days later, looking down over Zerna, it was a peaceful enough scene with people going about their work. Tina's voice floated up in the morning air, singing as always as she helped her mother with the housework. On a grassy hillside the cowbells tinkled as the children took the animals to graze. Suddenly the peace was shattered with a long burst of machine gun fire from a distant hilltop, accompanied by the crump of mortar bombs. As I looked in the direction of the noise, tracer bullets arced across the hills to a wood on the skyline and a column of black smoke curled up into the cloudless sky from a burning house. The partisans were being hunted and I knew from that moment that things would never be the same and that the time had come to carry out my plan to get to Rome. Certainly no one would ask me to leave and the decision would be entirely my own. This time, I would not be deflected from my intention. When I thought of the threat that my continued presence imposed on every family in the commune it was not difficult to make up my mind to leave immediately. The consequences of discovery at Zerna did not bear thinking about.

My feelings for the kindly mountain people went much deeper than mere friendship. I went down to seek Tina's father and saw that he was worried and uneasy. Telling him of my intentions, he slowly nodded his head and agreed that it would be best. Tina and Ross were in the kitchen and as usual seemed to have no sense of danger. After the months of excellent food and the exercise I had taken, I felt fit and well and quite capable of taking the long walk down through Italy. Pino said he would accompany me across the hills for a while to ensure that I was heading in the right direction and as we departed, Rosa pressed a small black silk purse into my hand, saying that I would need some money. Tina gave me a picture of the Madonna and a St Christopher medallion. It was an emotional farewell, I thanked all of them for their unstinted hospitality and Rosa was close to tears.

Chapter Six

A Long Walk South

Leaving the outskirts of the village, we agreed that Pino should walk some distance ahead. If we were stopped he would not then be directly in my company. Proceeding down the valley, we crossed a main road, then after a long climb, reached the top of the hill that I had seen from Zerna. Pino was looking tired and I insisted that he return. He carefully pointed out the route that I should take to the distant skyline and as we shook hands I thanked him warmly and asked him to thanks his friends for their kindness. He smiled and after a short embrace, turned and walked back down the mountain. At the last moment, we both waved a final farewell as I turned my back on Zerna.

Taking my first steps toward the uncertain future I found consolation in the fact that I no longer posed a threat to anyone else. It was as though a cloud had been lifted from me and I felt lighthearted and confident as I began my walk to the next range of hills. I hoped to make as much progress as possible and it was now passed midday. Hurrying through several small communities, I attracted a few curious looks from local people but no one challenged me. I wore civilian clothes and provided I did not speak, they would have no reason to be suspicious. I noticed that many of the houses seemed quite deserted with the families working out on the land. I did not want to make any detours across country, which were both time wasting and fatiguing, so I followed the narrow paths, keeping a sharp lookout for anyone is uniform.

In the late afternoon, thirst was becoming a problem and I realised that I would soon have to ask someone for water. As I walked on, I selected a house remote from the others and approached it through a small yard. Several chickens fled, squawking loudly, and an elderly man looked out from a doorway. He was frightened and puzzled by my sudden appearance, and on my asking for water, he pointed to a bucket in the kitchen. Suspicious, he asked where I had come from. He knew immediately that I was not Italian. When I explained my presence there, he seemed to relax, saying that he had been a soldier in the First World War, as had Pino. Like many other people I had met, he commented on the folly of the war, condemning the Fascists for the misery that they had brought upon Italy.

He opened a cupboard and produced a bottle of wine. As we toasted one another, a young woman came across the yard carrying a basket of vegetables. He introduced her as his daughter, Gina. She was a dark attractive girl with a pleasant personality, and as she busied herself preparing a meal, they said that I was welcome to share it with them. I had intended to push on, but the temptation to rest and enjoy a meal was too great and I succumbed to their kind invitation.

During the meal, which was most enjoyable, Gina disclosed that the Germans had conscripted her husband for forced labour, and she had no idea of his whereabouts. It seemed however remote people were, no one could escape the clutches of this conflict. I tried to offer some words of condolence and said that I was convinced that the war was coming to its end. My host raised his hands in a gesture of resignation, saying, "Who knows?" Later, when I was preparing to leave, he produced a bottle of the potent Grappa that I had tasted whilst living in Pino's outhouse. As I could not afford to stagger through the hills in a semi-conscious state. I politely declined his offer and asked for a glass of wine instead. Gino and her father had been more then generous and I decided to move on in spite of their invitation to remain with them overnight. Realising that I would need a drink, they provided me with a straw covered wine bottle filled with water, and with the aid of a piece of cord, I slung it over my back. I thanked them for their kindness and resumed my trek to the south.

After covering a few more miles of rough terrain, it became obvious that it would be dark before I could traverse the valley that stretched for miles in front, with no habitation in sight. I was on a thickly wooded hill and as it was high ground, I decided to settle down in my present position for the night rather than chance an accident in the darkness. I found a sheltered hollow below the skyline and collected sufficient branches and bracken to construct a rough shelter. There was no shortage of dead wood, and before dark I kindled a fire, cleaned my teeth and relaxed. It was a lovely night: not a breath of wind to stir the trees, with only the occasional crackle from the glowing embers to disturb the perfect silence. At that moment, I would have sold my soul for a mug of tea and a cigarette.

The past years began to reel through my mind like a cinema film and in an effort to keep my spirits up, I steered my thoughts to some of the more amusing things that had happened since my call up with the Terriers. One of the new recruits who joined our battery in the first few months of the war was such a huge man that although the quartermaster managed to fit him out with battledress uniform, he searched in vain for a hat to suit his head. Eventually a decision was taken to permit his wearing a civilian bowler on parade while they scoured neighbouring depots to sort out the problem. Standing head and shoulders over the rest of us, it was a strange spectacle for the Royal Regiment of Artillery, always renowned for an impeccable turnout, to have a boiler hatted soldier in their ranks, but after a few days, it was accepted as normal and he took part in gun drill without any embarrassment. During a visit from a Divisional Commander and his staff to watch us training, he suddenly vanished from our gun team. He had been spirited away into the battery office where he could work for a few ours without "The Hat". It would have been too much for our officers to display him wearing a gent's bowler on such an official occasion. He was a determined chap, and soon became an efficient gunner. We all missed him in the coming weeks when he was transferred to intelligence.

At about the same time, I developed an unpleasant rash on the inside of my leg. Reporting sick with a number of others, the Medical Officer diagnosed it as "Dhobi's Itch", an infection caused by the rough khaki chaffing on the skin. I was transported away with two other colleagues Ralph and Vic, to a mental hospital, part of which had been requisitioned for military use. For some reason, there was no room for us on the wards, and three iron beds were hastily erected in a padded cell, of all places. The walls and the door were quilted with black leather upholstery and there was a small barred window near the ceiling at the far end. We were young, and high spirited and my cell mates decided to act out the part. In the evening when a young trainee nurse appeared on the scene, doing her best to look primly efficient, the men romped about like demented apes, chasing the poor girl round the cell. She screamed in mock terror and joined in the fun. With me encouraging them, it made quite a din. Our antics were suddenly curtailed when a Sergeant Major of the Coldstream Guards filled the doorway with his massive frame. He was scarlet with rage, an impressive sight as he bellowed in his best parade ground voice for the benefit of the entire hospital, "You are soldiers now, not bloody clowns!" He added in an undiminished tone that the padded cell was the right place for us. Poor nurse Ruby fled past him into the corridor as our verbal lashing continued with the threat of dire punishment if there was a repetition of our un-soldierly behaviour. We were careful not to upset him again.

As the dying embers of my fire began to wink like eyes, I fell asleep wondering where Ralph and Vic were at the moment. In later years I discovered that Ralph had been released from military service to resume his work on engineering design while Vic had slogged through the jungles of Burma.

I awoke at first light, cold and damp from the heavy dew that had saturated my shelter. It was strangely quiet without the familiar dawn chorus of the countryside at home. Nothing stirred as I looked across the valley, and fixed on a landmark, which I judged to be southeast. I set off stiffly for the next summit, deliberating on how much longer my luck would hold out after all these months of wonderful freedom. It was pleasant to be walking downhill; it made the going so much easier. When I came upon a well-used track, progress was even better. I found myself at a small wooden bridge spanning a river, which although shallow was fast-flowing. It was an opportunity to wash and bathe my feet. The sun was easing away my overnight aches and pains. I examined my boots, they had endured remarkably well since the day I was issued with them, but they were not beginning to crack. I could only pray that somewhere I would encounter a friendly cobbler, who would refurbish the soles for me, although Pino had often said that leather was unobtainable.

I felt refreshed after my wash and made the steep climb towards my next objective. When I reached the top, the terrain stretched out before me flat and featureless. The only building of any sort was a stone shrine to the Madonna at the side of the path. It was quite usual to find these serene little monuments. This one, however, was by far the largest I had seen and provided refuge for the traveller against the elements. From one wall the Virgin smiled down benevolently. Fresh flowers had been placed in a receptacle at her feet. These places always seemed to instill a sense of well-being and comfort and I usually made a point of resting for a while whenever I saw one. Looking inside, I noticed that it was clean and dry with a wooden seat along each wall. Deep in thought, I walked some twenty yards further on. Suddenly my reverie was interrupted by a sharp command to stop. My heart sank out and I frantically sought some way of escape. My worst fears had been realised and I was trapped in the open with no cover to provide a way out. As I slowly turned, I saw two figures emerging from behind the shrine, both were uniformed and armed. I prayed inwardly that they were partisans and not a German patrol, but as they drew nearer I saw with dismay that they carried German weapons.

While one of the men kept his gun trained, the other began a search of my pockets, demanding to know where I was going and I attempted to bluff it out by saying that I was visiting friends some miles away. He found my army paybook and map of Italy and asked point blank if I was English. There seemed no point in denying it. I confessed that I was a British soldier and when they learned of my attention of getting to the front, they shook their heads telling me that not only was it too dangerous, but that I would not be allowed to proceed through their territory, without the approval of their commander. He would issue a permit if I could prove that my story was genuine. I was overjoyed to hear that they were Rebels, as the Fascist newspapers described them and the relief must have been evident on my face. They escorted me to their headquarters and I noticed that several other men had appeared in the vicinity. This led me to believe that it was an observation post for it commanded an excellent view of the whole surrounding area. No doubt they had watched my approach from the time that I had left the river. We arrived later at a small isolated commune after passing through several groups of men standing around laughing and chatting. My captors greeted them as though after a long absence. They all eyed me with curiosity. These men really looked the part: the way I had always pictured the partisans in my mind. Long haired and bearded with a whole variety of weapons both German and Italian, bandoliered and bulleted. Most of them had British hand grenades at their waists although I observed several German potato mashers as we called their stick bombs. Their attire ranged from city lounge suits to parts of captured German uniform and jackboots, and a large amount of Italian army green. One could not imagine a more motley crew. The bond that united them was an intense hatred of Fascists and Germans and the certain knowledge that they could expect no quarter if they were taken prisoner.

At the centre of the commune, we entered a cottage with a notice above the door stating that it was a police detachment. I was paraded before the commander who used the alias of "Jack". He was a stickily built man with black wavy hair and a short beard. He wore a dark green jacket and Sam Browne with a .38 revolver. He spoke English with a slight accent and his demeanour indicated that he was not someone to be trifled with. I could not understand how he had attained his position of authority in the organization. He resembled an officer of the Alpini, the crack Italian mountain fighters. Two other armed men were sitting at the side of the room and one came forward to empty my pockets and place the contents on the table. The map of Italy seemed to intrigue him and he asked if I was a German deserter, no doubt influenced by my fair complexion. He picked up my army paybook and I insisted that this was the only identification I could provide, my dog tags having long since disappeared. In the book under the section "distinctive marks" it said that there was a scar over my heart. He wanted to see this and was not impressed when shown. Next he discovered the German pamphlets that had been dropped on me and became all the more suspicious, asking how I came to have them. The three men found it hard to credit my story of the German plane. The details of my prison camp internment were written down, and those of my subsequent escape. He wanted the location of my hideout in the intervening months and the names of my helpers. I told them I could not reveal the names of my friends or details of their whereabouts and he thumped the table angrily, insisting that if they were my friends they were also his and perhaps one day he himself may seek a safe refuge. I persisted in my refusal on the grounds that information travelled fast through the mountains and I could put them in jeopardy.

They all conferred for a while in Italian and from the gist of their fast chatter, I realised that I was to be locked up. I was not prepared for this and now my freedom was again at stake with no means of proving that I was a bona-fide escapee. Clearly smarting over our verbal confrontation, and not accustomed to insubordination, the commander resented my refusal to cooperate with him. He began a long interrogation by producing a pack of American cigarettes from his drawer and inviting me to smoke. Noticing my surprise, he commented that they were able to get them occasionally.

We commenced with the usual rank, number and serial number followed by date and place of capture, my regiment and the name of my commanding officer. There was no option but to surrender this information in the name of my cause, but the subsequent questionnaire was much more subtle. He demanded the names of my civilian employers and those of two colleagues, my old school and two teachers and finally, my mother's maiden name. I though that this last was ingenious, and was able to provide all the answers without hesitation. After checking the details once more, I put my signature at the bottom of my sheet and he warned that all this would have to be verified. I assumed from this information that they were in contact with the allies, taking it for granted that my parents would be informed of my whereabouts. For some unknown reason, either security or neglect, the information was never passed on and the strain of my being posted as missing for the second time had been too much for them.

Several weeks later when a party of men passed through our area on a mission to allied lines, they agreed to take a hastily scribbled letter from me to the military authorities. They were as good as their word and delivered the note. Many weeks afterwards, the tattered remnant was pushed through my letterbox in London by an unknown courier, too late. Those missing weeks could have made all the difference.

After our lengthy interview, I was told that I would be allowed to stay outside under escort during the daylight hours, if I gave my word not to leave the area without permission. At night I would be confined to the police house. They were considerably friendlier now as I was taken to another house close by and placed in the care of the partisans in charge. To the relief of my fast shrinking stomach, I was provided with a large bowl of steaming macaroni stew. At that moment, it all seemed to be worthwhile and once again I felt I should thank my unseen protector.

After the meal, I was introduced to a partisan named Giuseppe who was to be my escort until I had been cleared by the security check. He was a pleasant young Neapolitan lad of about my own age. He had no knowledge of English and like Tuglio, was very keen to learn. We passed many hours in conversation, which benefitted us both and we became firm friends. I called him Joe. I was content to stay in the house for a few days, but later joined in some of the work around the commune. There was always plenty to do and after a while I became accepted as one of them. In one area of the camp, groups of armed, bearded men and several women were sitting around in the sun, laughing and joking. Behind them was an old millhouse with a massive waterwheel slowly turning in a foaming cascade of water. Gazing at that scene with all the men dressed in a variety of clothing. It seemed so unreal, reminiscent of a backcloth for a Hollywood operetta. The situation was real enough though, and these were all determined men, with everything to lose waiting for the signal to go into action with the advancing allies. Recently the Fascist newspapers had tried to seduce the partisan conscience by enticing to give themselves up under some sort of amnesty. The articles made a pretense of appealing to their compassionate sensitivities, saying that their families desperately needed them and stressing that the rigours of the approaching winter would be difficult and dangerous in the mountains, not to mention the threat of execution of handing them over. These inducements failed to have any effect. No one was influenced by these dubious Fascist promises.

Joe had worked for the railways before fleeing from the Nazis. He was an ardent Communist, declaring that they would take over the peace. Typically Neapolitan, he would often burst into song when we were out working. He had a lovely voice and appreciated me calling him "Caruso". Sometimes in the evening he would entertain us with the Neapolitan love songs, which I enjoyed so much. Someone would join in with a guitar, and after his heartrending version of "Mamma", I think most of us were close to tears.

I soon discovered that there were people here from all walks of life; school teachers, businessmen, musicians and teachers, but as the weeks passed the Communist influence became more pronounced.

While talking with the Commander one day, he confirmed something I had heard months ago. The prison camp was being used to confine civilians who had been brought from the South awaiting deportation to Germany. The ultimate fate of these poor unfortunate people was, of course, unknown to us at the time.

After several days, I was informed that I had been cleared by their security check, and the Commander said that I was free to leave, handing me a printed permit bearing his signature and an official stamp with the head of Garibaldi inset on a pointed star.

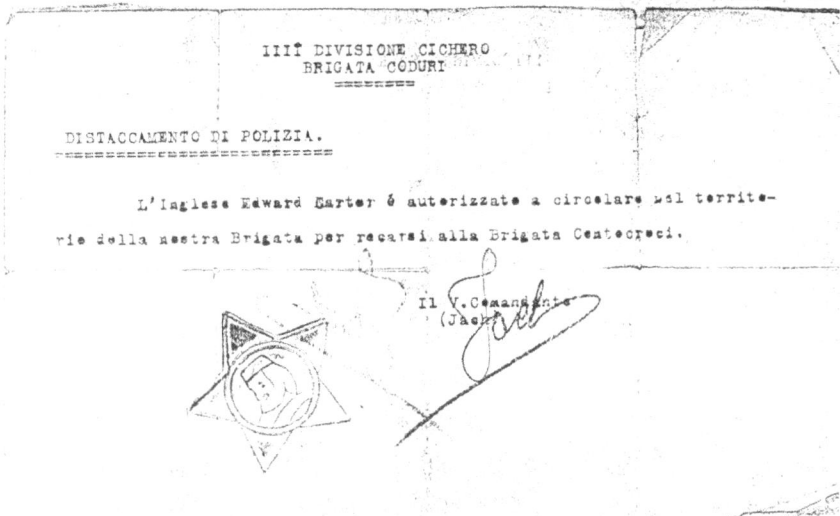

Translation: The Englishman Edward Carter is authorise to travel in our territory to go to rejoin the Brigade of a Hundred Crosses.

I had the option of becoming a member of the brigade or leaving and if I wanted their protection and food, he said that I would have to become one of them. I agreed, and the following day they presented me with a rifle and a grenade. There was only one snag, they had no ammunition and when I asked about this, they said it was on its way. I tested the bolt action of the rifle and saw that the weapon had been maintained in a clean condition and well oiled. However, it was with some regret that I took the arms. By contravening the Geneva Convention, I had revoked the right to protection and had in fact become a "France Tyreur". There was no going back now and I had to hope for the best. The Allies were advancing swiftly and it seemed to be the right decision to make at the time, but I could not foresee the disastrous consequences of the oncoming winter, which kept the Allies bogged down until the spring. With the war in its final stages I desperately wanted to survive.

The Brigade maintained several small units some distance from the base as observation posts to watch the main roads. There was every possibility of sudden raids and a strict vigil was kept. For several weeks I took my turn with the others doing the same job that I had with the gunners. By this time I had been issued with just twelve rounds of ammunition. It was the early days of the movement and they had to rely on hit and run tactics, sparing as much ammunition as they could. But the organisation was fast growing and would later be a force to be reckoned with.

My first operational role as a fully paid up member of the gang was to assist in an airdrop of supplies some distance away in the hills. We were about twenty strong and set out at first light. We found our way to a plateau high in the mountains where contact was made with another brigade. After much discussion among the people in charge, markers were laid out for some distance and we retired to a farmhouse to await developments. It was around midday that the ground began to shake with the sounds of approaching aircraft. As we dashed out I witnessed a most impressive sight. A long line of American Air Force Dakotas swept towards us with a fighter escort. As each one passed a mass of coloured parachutes blossomed out to the cheers of the waiting partisans. It was a wonderful moment. The containers were spread right across the plateau and we surged forward to recover them and manhandle the precious cargo to the farmhouse. It was heavy work over the rough ground and with the last one retrieved, the parachutes were carefully folded and spirited away to be bisected and sold on the black market to provide food and dresses for the city women who could afford to pay a very high price for them.

As the last Dakota vanished across the hills, the fighters roared past dipping their wings to acknowledge our waves. With the possibility of a German raid, no time was wasted in dividing the spoils. Everyone wanted to get away as quickly as possible. Many of the containers were taken away by mule and the rest broken open to be emptied of sten guns, explosives, blankets, tinned food and masses of ammunition. Most of it was to be transported to a central depot far away from the dropping zone. However, to my surprise and joy when one of the casks was opened it contained dozens of pairs of British Army boots and it seemed as though my prayers of several weeks ago had been answered. They had literally dropped from heaven.

There was quite an argument when I began to sort out a pair of my size and an acting quartermaster told me to leave them alone. I was quick to point out that they came from my country and I intended to have them. It was an ugly moment and in the heat of our exchange, I was afforded another surprise by the sudden appearance of a British major in full army uniform wearing a black beret. I explained the situation and showed him my tattered boots. He immediately sanctioned my demand, ignoring the mutterings of the others. I later discovered that he belonged to the SOE and was in command of the whole operation. He also gave me a packet of American cigarettes, which helped to calm my ruffled feathers. As he was about to leave, he said that a directive had been issued to all partisan groups to pass escaped prisoners down through their territories and to give them assistance to the front. He also provided me with a pin pricked map showing a safe route, which gave the impression that he had been working behind the lines for some time. At my request to accompany him, he said it was not possible and advised me to make my way south. I was grateful for his intervention and later learned that his name was Major Lett.

My first taste of real action came when a large party of us set out to obtain food supplies from scattered farms. This involved crossing the main road, always a hazard, and on the way down we split into two groups. Some time later when we had almost reached the highway, a burst of small arms and machine gun fire came from the direction of the other group. Making our way round to them we saw a cluster of German vehicles some distance away, and the partisan fire was being returned. They observed our approach and directed a hail of fire towards us as they began to move. It was a heated exchange while it lasted and our ammunition was exhausted. They were out of range for hand grenades and we had to watch them drive away. Our party carried on to join up with the others and I was surprised to see that they escorted a prisoner, a German officer. He had been captured while cycling along the road and they were taking him back, cycle as well.

There had been no casualties in our groups and on reaching the commune the captive was taken to a house under close guard. They wasted no time in letting him know that I was English and as we viewed each other with some curiosity I found that I could not muster up any burning hatred towards him. If anything I felt sympathy. He was an officer of the Wehrmacht, tall, rangy and every inch a soldier, typical of the African Corps men that I had grown to respect for their humane treatment of prisoners. There was camaraderie in the desert with Rommel's men and I do not believe it existed in other theatres of war.

The German sat at the table, quietly smoking. It was clear that his fate hung in the balance but his face was impassive, showing no signs of emotion. He was a brave man who would not have pleaded for his life to be spared. Guerilla warfare prevailed in the mountains without the Geneva Convention to protect the participants under international rules. Captured partisans expected no clemency and many of the men related harrowing stories of friends and families who had suffered greatly at the hands of Germans and Fascists. Their hostile attitude towards the prisoner was understandable yet killing in battle was something quite different from a cold-blooded execution. As I glanced towards the captive, our eyes met and for a fleeting moment, I sensed a bond of sympathy between us. After all, I had been captured by these very people and was constrained to point out that I had been treated with courtesy and respect when I had been taken prisoner. The assembled partisans discussed which course of action should be taken and the outlook for the German officer began to look grim. Later in the evening, we were all relieved when someone in authority took a decision that an attempt would be made to exchange him for captured resistance men. That night he was locked in a wooden outhouse and by morning, had escaped leaving a gaping hole in the rear wall.

There was to be no more ammunition for my rifle and after cleaning it, I handed it back to the person in charge of the store who promised a sten gun when it became available. At that time, the Communists at a higher level were salting weapons away, not with the intention of using them against the Germans but to win the peace. With the Allied advance progressing rapidly, it was wrongly assumed that the end was imminent in Italy.

Some of the men were planning to visit a nearby town and much against my better judgement, I accepted their invitation to go along. At a small studio on the outskirts of the town, we posed for a group photograph, and although we were not armed, it showed us as a fine gang of desperados. After this, we filed into a barber's shop and from the tone of their greetings, it seemed that some of the men were acquainted with the elderly hairdresser, although I thought it best not to be inquisitive. He was interested to discover that I was English and asked me many questions about London. While he worked, he casually mentioned that there was a police barracks at the other end of the town, which made me reflect that this trip would be rather foolhardy. I was relieved, therefore, when we departed for the hills after having a few drinks. We took several newspapers back and bottles of wine for the others. The friendly barber provided me with a small bar of soap, a commodity that was unobtainable in the shops at the time. The official issue soap resembled a block of stone that gave no lather at all. I had a terrible dread of becoming lousy again and took every opportunity to wash my underclothes and shirt in boiling water. The soap would be invaluable in preventing any further infestation.

I had not seen Joe for several days and when I did, he told me that the brigade was to be visited by a high ranking Commander of the partisan movement. The following day, when news of his approach reached us, we turned out in full force to await his arrival. We were about eighty strong and we lined up as the party came into view. There were four men on horseback. The leading rider was a small mustachioed figure, wearing a large broad-brimmed hat and flowing black cloak. The quartet plodded through our silent ranks and someone whispered reverently that this was "Il Lupo", "The Wolf". With an inward chuckle and not quite so reverently, I noticed a marked resemblance to the newspaper cartoonist's popular image of a Trotsky anarchist, usually pictured holding a smoking bomb. The truth was that he had the reputation of a brave resistance fighter who had earned the respect of all the partisans. They dismounted at the police house where "Jack" awaited them.

There were rumours of impending action, and we soon discovered from this visit that the Germans had asked for a truce with the mountain fighters. In the last few months, they had lost several thousand men in other sectors where the brigades were stronger and better armed, and now with the American Fifth Army advancing towards us, and the British Eighth making good progress on the Adriatic front, the German Commander had asked for his troops to be allowed to withdraw unhindered through the hills. His request had been refused and it was thought that they would take reprisals.

We began to get more supplies and I was at last provided with a sten gun, but as usual, ammunition was rationed. Compared with the Thompson sub-machine gun that I was accustomed to in artillery it appeared cheap and crude, but there was no doubting its efficiency. I was also shown a box of explosives: imitation horse dung, which was intended to damage vehicles. It was quite new to me and seemed a good idea. The Commander called me to his office one afternoon saying that a large funeral ceremony was to take place some miles away. Patrol activity was increasing on both sides and several partisans had been killed in clashes with the enemy. They were to be buried with military honours and he was sending a party of six from our brigades. He asked if I would like to attend and I replied that it would be an honour and a privilege. I understand that several nationalities were to be represented and Jack suggested with a broad grin, that I "go for Churchill" as I would probably be the only Englishman. We shared a laugh when I said that I could also use one of his cigars at that moment. At my request, he agreed that Joe could be included in the group, and the next day, we set out across the hills.

After a walk of some distance, we came to a pleasant site at the foot of a gently sloping hillside, bordered with trees. An altar had been set up at one side and the bodies of partisans were draped with the Italian National colours. The Red Flag was also prominently featured. Nature had provided a golden day for this memorable occasion, and the sun glinted on the falling leaves as hymns were sung and a soft breeze carried the silvery tribute of the bugles through the silent hills. Far below, the Mediterranean curved it's way into the haze of Southern France where the Americans had battled through the Champagne country. The congregation was some three hundred strong and many people from the surrounding villages mingled with the partisans to form an impressive scene on this autumn day. I was somewhat relieved when the ceremony ended and we began disperse. Although the Allies controlled the skies, a single enemy fighter on the prowl could have caused many casualties.

With the movement of the crowd, I had lost contact with the others and when I located them, they were in conversation with a group of Yugoslavian partisans. These were Tito's fighters and their smart uniform contrasted sharply to our somewhat disheveled appearance. We were aware of their heroic struggle against the Nazis and all held them in great regard. With their tanned, leathery faces they gave the appearance of a formidable group of warriors, but I was puzzled by their appearance and it was only when I noticed the soft curve of their tunics that I realised several were in fact women.

I engaged them in conversation and found that we could understand each other in Italian. I learned from one of them that she had been fighting for two years. When she realised that I was English, her face broke into a broad smile as she said "Bravo Churchill" and when I responded with "Vivo Tito" she gave a soft laugh that was pleasantly feminine. I mused that in peacetime and wearing a summery dress, she would have been very attractive. But the hands, which carried the machine gun, looked strong and capable, leaving me in no doubt that she could use it as expertly as any of her male comrades.

After talking to them for a considerable time, it became apparent that it was too late to think of returning and Joe said that we would be able to stay the night. Together with the Yugoslavians, we trooped to the outskirts of a small village where another brigade had established their headquarters, and were shown to a barn. It was clean and roomy, with straw mattresses piled at one end, and I noticed with some interest that a radio transmitter had been set up in one corner. After settling down and making ourselves comfortable, I was pleased to see baskets of food being brought in, with bottles of wine. While we were eating, the bottles of rough mountain wine were passed around from mouth to mouth as we toasted each other in a variety of languages. The commander had been right about several nationalities being represented, and I understood there were Poles and French as well as the Yugoslavians. I was the only Englishman. As darkness fell, oil lamps were lit and more people crowded in until all the floor space was taken up. Someone handed round a carton of Italian Nationale cigarettes, which were very pungent, but most welcome. The air began thick as we huddled together and I became sandwiched among Tito's women fighters. Although we were not very comfortable, at least we were warm, and I fell asleep with one of them blowing into the back of my neck. I had slept under many strange conditions during the past few years and I felt that this particular occasion would be the one I would never forget.

The next day we were awake at first light and it was a relief to get outside away from the crush of sweaty bodies. Our Yugoslavian friends were making their way to the north and we wished each other "Buona Fortuna" as they left. After thanking our hosts, we started the return journey, hoping to find something to eat on the way back at one of the small communities, and we were lucky enough to have a meal provided for us.

When we arrived, the others were interested to know about the funeral and our encounter with the Yugoslavians. It was some weeks later that we received the distressing news from a group of partisans who came from inland that there had been a massive German raid on their stronghold. It unfolded that for some reason they had relaxed their usual strict vigilance and were taken by surprise in a sudden night attack mounted by the SS and their Mongol mercenaries. They moved in at first light and succeeded in encircling the whole area. In the ensuing four days they not only decimated the partisans, but also brutally murdered hundreds of civilians. There had been men, women and children of all ages. The final death toll was put at eighteen-hundred. The entire area was devastated and abandoned as a smouldering ruin. The few survivors were completely stunned. It was one of the worst atrocities of the war, but somehow the awful truth seemed to have become submerged in the tidal wave of death and destruction that was sweeping across Europe at the time. There were many harrowing reports of brutality and murder. It was hard to determine the true facts from political propaganda. Later, the true story was described in all its lurid and terrible detail and many years later by American author Jack Olsen in his book *Silence on Monte Sole* (Arthur Barker Limited, London, 1969).

After the war, the German Commander of the raiding troops was jailed for life, but he was later released from a Naples prison in 1985 into Austria after serving forty years of his sentence. This was against the wishes of the survivors, who had petitioned several times for clemency but had always refused a pardon. It was stated at his trial that he refuted the number of deaths by saying it was "only" six hundred.

As the mild autumn weather changed with the approach of winter, I became increasingly aware of my lack of warm clothing. I had not really thought about it until now. As on my previous occasions I had hoped that something would turn up, and perhaps the next airdrop would bring something useful. To make matters worse it was said that the Allies would be bogged down and unable to make any decisive advance until the Spring offensive, which was at least five months away. The prospect of spending another Winter indoors in the mountains was very daunting, but strangely enough, something did turn up.

At the end of November, the partisans suffered a devastating blow from General Alexander's HQ advising them to disband and return to their homes. It was unbelievable after the danger and privation that they had faced in their struggle against the Germans and the Fascists. We had poised for a final showdown with the enemy, and now a cloud of despondency hung over us with the prospect of having to wait several more months. To be told to lay down their arms and return to certain arrest and possible execution instead of being liberated and free was shattering indeed and quite inexplicable. The feeling was one of complete disbelief, and I felt considerably embarrassed. Strong words were used about the British, although the men were generous enough not to vent their anger on me. The official reason given for this directive was that there could be no more supplies due to the Winter, but the underlying motive was the Allies' fear of the growing strength of the Communists, whose declared intention it was to take over the peace. Several days later in the Commander's office, I was informed that the order to despatch all escaped prisoners to the south had been repeated without exception. The decision to leave had been made for me, and with mixed feelings, I agreed to go, the dream of marching with the partisans in a victory parade through the city now gone.

With Christmas only three weeks away, I thought that it would be the most favourable time to get across the strongly fortified Gothic Defence Line, spanning the country from east to west. When the time came for my departure, the brigade gave me a good send off, offering all kinds of good and bad advice. They also gave me a bag of food and a bottle of wine. I handed back my sten gun and hand grenade and Joe wrote down the address of his parents in Naples. It was yet another of those poignant moments. Since my escape, I had known so many outstanding characters who would remain forever in my thoughts. I reflected what might become of them all. I knew that I would remember them for the rest of my days; Pino grinning over his home brewed "Whiskey", Tuglio fumbling with his English, little Enzio glued excitedly to his radio, Tony working at his baskets, the Commander, bearded and handsome with questioning eyes, the elderly priest who had shared his lonely meal with me and given up his bed for the comfort of a passing fugitive, old twinkle-eyed Luigi with his wrinkled face and Texas drawl, "we'll look after you son" and also there was Giuseppe with his Neapolitan "Canzone d'Amore". I would never forget them, the people of those memorable years.

Chapter Seven

My Best Christmas Present

With the help of others, I selected a point on the distant horizon to aim for, and set off from our mountain eerie towards the war zone. As I crossed the valley, I looked back and waved a last farewell. At the bottom, I had to cross the main road where we had captured the German officer, and had to wait until several enemy trucks swept past before starting the long climb to the next peak. It was late afternoon when the rain began, quickly drenching me, and with no available shelter, there was no option but to squelch to the top of the hill. From this summit I could see a farmhouse in the next valley. There was no one about as I climbed into a hay-filled loft above the cowshed. I stripped off my saturated clothes and gratefully relaxed naked in the soft sweet hay. Taking the wet maps from my pocket and spreading them out to dry, I found the photograph of the partisans and realised how damning it could be. There was every chance of recapture as I neared the Front, and I pushed it behind the rafters before settling down to tuck into the bread and sausage that the men had given me. When darkness fell, sleep came easily as I listened to the nocturnal creatures scurrying about while the cow gently lowed and stamped her feet. It seemed that I had barely closed my eyes when the sound of someone calling out awoke me with a start. Crawling to the door, I saw that it was a sunny morning and an elderly woman in black was feeding her chickens. When she began to approach the barn, I decided to make my presence known and called out to her. She was rather startled, but listened as I explained that I had been caught in the storm. She returned to the house reappearing with her husband who carried a blanket. He was short, thick-set man and he climbed into the loft. As we chatted I was asked once more if I was a German deserter. I convinced him with my army pay-book and partisan pass that I was British, whereupon he introduced himself as Benito. Wrapped in the blanket, I was accompanied to the house, where they made up a massive fire on the kitchen floor. Crouching low to avoid the choking smoke, Benito and I talked about the war as his wife prepared bread and milk for us and hung my clothes to dry.

At their invitation, I stayed for the next three days. The trousers and underclothes dried, but the jacket remained wet, and Benito generously provided me with another, and a woollen pullover. I asked for a pencil and paper and wrote a receipt with my name and number, describing their kind help, and urged them to present it to the military authority after the liberation. They were adamant that no reward was necessary, but I insisted that they accept it, stressing the importance of keeping it well hidden until the Germans had gone. After thanking them, I resumed my trek through the mountains with a new strength, fortified with good food and dry clothes.

I felt ready for the next stage, and at this point could hear the rumble of distant gunfire. Late in the afternoon, I approached a small village at the bottom of a valley, which resembled a small English community, with a scattering of bungalows and one main thoroughfare. I watched for a while from a clump of trees, making sure there were no signs of German activity, and apart from the occasional military vehicle, the place seemed to be quite deserted. I had intended to pass straight through, but could not resist the temptation to get a drink at the bar, and peering through a side window, I saw three men conversing with a woman behind the counter. They were all civilians, and as I entered, the talk stopped abruptly, and the three moved to a corner table. The atmosphere was tense as I asked for a drink; my appearance and my bad Italian puzzled all of them. Trying to look unconcerned, although I felt very apprehensive, I sat down and occasionally glimpsed an inquiring face peeping at me from a door at the rear. Something seemed not quite right with the trio. Two of them wore trilby hats and their faces were quite rosy, which was unusual for Italians. The third was a big man with a sallow face, black curly hair and a moustache. Behind the bar, the person seemed to be a homely looking buxom woman with a pleasant enough face, but she was clearly ill at ease. After some twenty minutes or so, she could no longer contain her curiosity and came to take my glass, asking if I required anything else. Lowering her voice, she declared that I was not Italian and began to probe about my presence in the village. I confessed that I was on the run, making my way to the front, and answered all her questions to her satisfaction, showing my papers. When I asked if she could put me up for the night, she called her husband, who had kept out of her way until now. As we chatted, it was my turn to be surprised. Nodding towards the three silent men, he said that they were South Africans who had escaped from a POW camp in the north. The atmosphere changed immediately as the ice was broken and they introduced themselves. The big man was Peter, a swarthy African, and his companions were Don and Syd. They had been staying there for the last five days and were all understandably alarmed at my arrival and the possibility of my being a German. People's lives were at stake and all strangers that appeared had to be regarded with suspicion. We recounted our various experiences, exchanging home addresses, and at nightfall, the four of us slept upstairs in a massive bed, only removing our boots in case we had to make a quick exit.

They were interested in my maps and we agreed to travel together after signing our names on a letter of commendation and thanks to our hosts so that they could be compensated. We began another long uphill climb to start our journey in the bright morning sunshine. We split into two groups at Peter's suggestion, he and I leading the way and the other two followed behind at some two hundred yards distance. In the event of trouble it would give them a chance to get away. It grew colder as we reached the snow line, but the exertion of plodding knee deep made up for the lack of warm clothing. Our progress was slow, but after the peak, conditions improved and we left the difficult stretch behind. At the valley floor we had to make a detour to find a way across a river. After some time, we discovered a wire contraption with a suspended pulley seat, which enabled us to cross one at a time. In the evening we again found shelter, huddling round a warm fire for the night.

It was in the foothills the next day that we came upon a tragedy. What had once been a happy mountain community had been reduced to a blackened, charred ruin, and the bitter stench of scorched timber reached us long before we saw the devastation. The few cottages that were not completely gutted were badly damaged, and as we took in the dreadful scene, faces peered from the depths of the blackened rooms, stunned and frightened. An old man stumbled out, sobbing with anguish, and his tormented eyes filled with tears as he blurted out the details of the terrible events that had taken place. The Germans had launched a reprisal raid against the partisans who had occupied the area and as usual the innocents had suffered, with four hundred villagers being murdered. The few who had escaped the carnage were in a state of shocked disbelief, and as we walked among the ruins, there seemed little we could do to offer any comfort. We could not forget those haunted faces. The name of the commune burned into my memory, "Vinca".

In the course of the next few miles, we roped in another Allied fugitive. We stopped again in a remote commune high in the mountains and were invited to the home of an English-speaking villager. He gave us a meal and after assuring himself that we were genuine, he produced what he called his "Surprise". He disappeared for some twenty minutes and returned with a young man wearing a leather jacket, announcing that this was Robert, an American fighter pilot who had been shot down in the north and passed down the escape route by the partisans. Although in some pain with a back injury, he was determined to carry on now that we were so close to the front.

Later in the evening when our host learned that I lived in London, he enquired if I knew the area of Shepherd's Bush, which was quite close to my home. He then named a small Italian restaurant that was owned by his brother and laughed delightedly when I said that I had dined there occasionally after swimming at the nearby Lime Grove pool. It was hard to believe – a small world indeed. When we left the following morning I promised to deliver a letter to his brother, after stressing that he use only Christian names and leave out his address. Eventually, I collected four such letters from various people along the way to relatives in England, and managed to deliver them all.

As we made our way through the mountains, we each picked up a small piece of marble for a keepsake and penciled our names on them. When I wrote to the men after the war, I was glad to hear that they had all reached safety. Now our most daunting obstacle was going to be the German Gothic Line, beyond which we could hear the sounds of battle. Further south, the American Fifth and the British Eighth armies had long since breached the Gustav and Adolph Hitler lines and were now just short of the Gothic. With Don in the lead, and in single file, we progressed along a narrow ledge with a sheer drop beneath. Far below, I observed several naked bodies lying by the side of the river. Following some yards behind him, I was dismayed to see the path had crumbled away, leaving only a shelf on which to get a foothold. Don was feeling his way along, clinging to the face with some twenty yards to teach safety, and with others closing up behind me, there was no option but to follow. My stomach turned over, and I felt sick digging my nails into the earthy face and clutching at bits of vegetation. A few yards along I froze and I panicked, pressing my face into the hillside, too petrified to go any further. I became aware of Peter's presence beside me, and realising what had happened, he advised me to remain still until I had recovered. His calming influence restored my confidence and he encouraged me to proceed slowly and when I saw that Don had reached safety it helped me to unfreeze but it was a nasty moment. Had I been alone I think I would have turned back and tried to find another way round. It was only Peter's help that got me across that fearful ledge. Some miles later, Don and I reached a grassy bank. We waited for the others to catch up as they were a long way back out of sight. It was Don who first spotted the patrol advancing towards us from further down the hillside.

The trees had shed their leaves and there was no cover. Hoping that we had not been spotted, we raced back to warn the others and scattered to find suitable hiding places. Don and I found a gulley and as the green uniforms of the Alpini moved silently on, he grinned and cocked an imaginary revolver towards them. He was always a cool character, never showing any signs of panic. We watched them climb the hill and out of sight before we regrouped to move on, it had the effect of making us more vigilant. Up to this moment we had rather been complacent, and it was agreed to keep to the low ground using all available cover although it would mean making wild detours. In the next two days, we reached the theatre of war.

We approached a small village in the late afternoon and observed from a vantage point a number of civilians but no sign of military presence. After watching for a time, Peter and I went to investigate while the others remained in cover. We saw smoke coming from the door of one house, and with the hope of getting a meal, we cautiously approached and saw a group of men sitting round a log fire. Our sudden appearance did not seem to startle them in the way that we had come to expect in other places. They waved to us to join them and we soon realised that they were all on the run for various reasons, waiting for the Allies to liberate them. Judging by the sound of battle, they were hoping that it would not be very long. A heavily built man wearing a trilby, whom they addressed as "Berto" appeared to be in charge. He expressed no surprise when we said that we were escaped prisoners. He told us that a large number of refugees were hiding out in the area, including many Jewish people, all scattered in various hideouts and praying for the British and Americans to arrive, but as Berto pointed out, there was little chance of that before the New Year.

With so many fugitives in the area, there was a great shortage of food, but in the general feeling of tension and uncertain future, hunger became of secondary importance compared with the fear of being recaptured so close to freedom. We managed to get a small meal of polenta, made with maize and a drink of wine and Berto handed round a pack of American cigarettes. While we enjoyed a smoke, he told us that he had crossed the Gothic Line several times guiding small groups of escapees through the hazards of the German defences. We gathered that he was in the pay of the Allied escape organisation. He had been conscripted for forced labour along with many local people and like myself had escaped to avoid deportation to Germany. When Peter asked for his help to escort us to safety, he said that it would not be until after Christmas, which was just a few days away.

In the morning, he took us to a hilltop and using his walking stick, carefully pointed out the safest route across the distant hills, but we were not encouraged when he spoke of minefields and concrete gun emplacements, which he had been forced to work on. We estimated that the ridge we would have to negotiate was some six miles away and after some discussion, Peter with the others decided to start out in the afternoon and cross during the night. I urged for them to wait for Christmas Eve, which would surely be the most advantageous time, and cross over on Christmas Day but they were all keyed up with the scent of freedom in the air and were very impatient to go. They would not heed the logic of my point of view. Although Berto agreed with me, we were unable to dissuade them. For me, after coming through so much, I had no intention of making a false move now with freedom so near at hand. Robert, the American, hesitated for a while, then with a rueful smile chose to throw in his lot with the others and hope for the best.

It was agreed that they should go two at a time, and as we deliberated, the air vibrated with the roar of the aircraft. A one thousand bomber raid thundered overhead to the north and Germany. The four men set out and we watched them disappear into the distance. With a final wave, I returned to the village with Berto. He allowed me to stay in the kitchen until the time came for me to leave on Christmas Eve, and stretching out on the floor I was able to stay underneath the choking smoke. This seemed to be a permanent feature of the cottages that had no chimney, and although it was hard, at least I was keeping warm and dry. Berto warned me to be alert to the danger of sudden raids by German patrols searching for deserters, stressing that they arrived quickly and without warning. Wandering around the village I made the acquaintance of several people of different nationalities and every barn and outhouse seemed to be occupied by forlorn little groups of people, cold and hungry with bewildered children who could not understand why they were living that way. But it was happening right across Europe with families uprooted and millions fleeing for their lives from the wave of terror as opposing armies fought savagely to the bitter end. This was the civilised world of 1944.

While at Berto's, I became friendly with a Pole and a Yugoslavian and invited their opinion about making an attempt to cross on Christmas Eve, but they declined my suggestion to make the journey together, having no illusions about their fate if we were captured. When the time came for me to leave, I thanked Berto for his help and set off in the afternoon. After covering several miles, a squadron of American fighters screamed across the valley, strafing the hilltop ahead of me and I decided to lay low for a while until after dark. It was a long climb to the ridge and although there was no moon I was able to pick my way along slowly, making as little noise as possible. The front was deathly quiet after the noise of the past few days and any little sound that I made seemed to be amplified by the silence. I edged towards the place where the planes had struck and rested in a clump of vegetation. I estimated the time to be about midnight. I lay in the eerie silence and thought of past Christmas Eves, hanging stockings up and roasting chicken and the smell of cigars. This would be one Christmas I would never forget.

There were not many hours left to daybreak and I had to move on. Removing my boots, I strung them round my neck. The ground was hard and the stones painful but I was moving silently towards the top of the ridge. Suddenly, I caught the unmistakable tang of tobacco smoke. My instincts were so keen that I was able to detect the slightest sound or smell and as the scent drifted on the clear night air from the right, I realised that I was not alone and slipped into my cover a few feet from the top. As I waited, I was haunted by the spectre of being taken prisoner again, and was determined not to make a hasty move. After a few minutes, I became aware of someone approaching and as I froze like a hunted animal, a group of shadowy figures padded silently past, melting away into the darkness, betrayed only by the rustle of their clothing. I had been lucky and had it not been for that tobacco scent, it could have ended in disaster or recapture.

I waited for some time and crawled to the top. The terrain ahead descended in a long slope and I knew that this was the place which had been so prominent in my thoughts over the past few months: no mans land between the Germans and the American Fifth Army. I had no way of guessing the time, but thought there could not be many more hours of darkness and I would have to get across the valley before dawn broke.

Crouching low as I moved over the skyline, I stumbled across the ridge for some thirty yards and plunged down the slope. There was no sound as I moved quickly towards what I could only hope that would be the American lines. Some way further down I came upon a mass of weapons abandoned over a wide area. Picking my way carefully through them, I noticed that they were Italian rifles and hand grenades. I kept down for a while, watching for any sound or movement in the strange silence of the predawn. Daylight was breaking as I reached the bottom to begin the climb to the next hilltop. This would be the most hazardous part as I lost the cover of darkness. Replacing my boots, I moved at a stumbling trot upwards. I could see a cottage behind a hedge some way off, and with no place to hide; there was no option but to carry on. I planned to reach the house and stay under cover during the daylight hours. After what seemed like an eternity, I crawled to the hedge and peered straight into the broad grin of a black face beneath a GI steel helmet. I had made it!

Chapter Eight

Back To Blighty!

The GI was a massive man. He reached over and dragged me across the hedge by the lapels. Filled with emotion, I collapsed to the ground, almost in tears as he wished me "Merry Christmas, man". He said that I was sure goddam lucky" to have crossed that open ground and had it not been Christmas Day I would not have made it. He felt sure that the Germans had observed my progress after daybreak and could only presume that they were being generous for "Natale", (Christmas)

The GI pointed to the cottage and crouching behind the hedge I made my way over to where the officer in charge examined my papers, asking for any useful information I may have gathered whilst behind German lines. On telling him about the group that had preceded me a few days before, he was keen to know about the American pilot whom I only knew as "Robert". He took down all the details of their route. Afterwards we enjoyed a Christmas breakfast and American cigarettes whilst he arranged transport to the rear with a group of casualties. It was a lengthy jeep ride to the coastal town of Via Reggio where I was handed over to the American Military Police who grilled me closely about my escape and military service. This was followed by a medical examination and close scrutiny of the area under my arms, which I assumed was a check for lice. I discovered some time later that they were looking for a tattooed blood group which was a feature of the elite German army units, enabling transfusions to be carried out quickly in the field.

After the interrogation, I was taken to a back street where several marquees had been set up as a cleansing centre for the troops. I enjoyed the full procedure of haircut, shower and complete change of clothing to emerge as a GI in a new uniform. It was so good to be clean again and as we made our way to the dining hall for Christmas dinner with the boys, I was told that I would be confined at night under guard until my identity had been verified. At the table, I found the GIs to be friendly and easy to get on with but I could only eat a small portion of the large Yuletide meal. For the rest of the afternoon there were plenty of drinks and smokes. On hearing of my escape the GIs were keen to know how I avoided capture and passed through the lines. As we left the hall in the evening, a ragged little group of urchins were scrabbling in the waste bins for something to satisfy their hunger on the Christmas Day of 1944. They begged for cigarettes, which could be sold on the black market and suggested that we should see their "pretty sister".

The American Military Police had taken over the local Police station and as I was locked in a cell for the night, I felt that being jailed for a while could hold no terrors for me after achieving my aim in reaching Allied lines. As I relaxed on a bunk, my thoughts went back to the people in the mountains huddled in barns and sheds, desperately trying to survive the long winter of privation and fear. Although it was cold in the cell with only one blanket, I reflected on my good fortune and how lucky I had been to come through unscathed. But in spite of the wine I had shared with the GIs, sleep would not come and I spent a restless night with my thoughts flitting over the past few weeks.

After a few days, the inactivity seemed to be telling on me and I longed to be on the move again. It was a relief when I heard that my identity had been verified and I joined a truckload of GIs going on leave to Florence when I rejoined the British army. Once again the inevitable interrogation when for the first time I was able to reveal the names and location of my benefactors in the mountains. I was assured that they would be compensated eventually. The letters for relatives in England were scrutinised and I was allowed to keep them. I was soon issued with a British uniform and paraded in the morning with several other men who told similar tales of escape as we each recounted our experiences.

A grim faced Sergeant of the Military Police put us through an inspection and with a short period of marching drill, bellowing that we "had got to learn how to be soldiers again!" He was furious when he spotted a tiny brass bell in my tie, which had been given to me by a gracious Italian lady in the mountains, with a little prayer for my safe passage across the front line at Christmas. As he roared "take it out!' I suddenly wished that I was back in the hills with the partisans, but in retrospect, I realised that the discipline was good for our physical and mental health in that we had no time for brooding and self-pity.

In the evening, we went to a local bar and shared a drink with men of the American Fifth Army and the British Eighth who had endured the long bloody slog through the mountains to the south, routing Hitler's toughest fighting men from their strongholds in the hills at great cost in casualties and privation. We felt proud to be with them and for a while the war was forgotten among the soldiers of a dozen different nationalities.

At last our future was arranged and the group was transported to Naples on American lorries where we boarded the troopship "Britannic" bound for England. A few days later, as we caught our first glimpse of "Blighty shores", a strange silence seemed to descend on the returning warriors, each one pensive with his own thoughts, after the years spent in foreign parts. The blood and sweat was behind us but for many the tears were yet to come with broken marriages, devastated homes and the loss of loved ones. As we filed ashore at a Scottish port, there was a short welcome speech by a Brigadier before boarding a train for London for a repatriation camp. Not knowing what to expect after such a long absence, it was with some apprehension that I queued to telephone a close neighbour to inform my parents of my safe return. The joy of setting foot on British soil again after four years was quickly snatched away when she bluntly said that they were both dead.

After the anticipation of a happy reunion, I was shocked and stunned but realised that the constant anxiety and strain of five years of war had taken its toll. With a heavy heart, I scarcely noticed the journey through the English countryside to the camp where I stayed for a few days and composed myself sufficiently to face the return home. It was a relief to find that my brother was on leave from the fighting front in Germany and together with his wife, we enjoyed a little celebration. The hastily scrawled letter I had sent while with the partisans many months before had indeed arrived, but too late. A doctor once told me that it was not possible to die of a broken heart and although he was right in the clinical sense, tragedy had shattered the lives of many millions throughout the world during those fateful years.

I went to see the parents of my friend Jim and heard of his whereabouts in German captivity. They were pleased to see me and I explained how it had not been possible for us to escape together but I had hoped that he would have been able to make a break before reaching the station. I sent a postcard to him from London to inform the others that I had reached home, albeit somewhat late. The letters I had brought from Italy were all duly delivered and relatives were very grateful.

In the next few days, I began to hear of the fate of my friends and for such a small community the casualties among my old gang had been high; Alec Prouse killed at Arnhem, Charlie West killed in an air raid, Jim Cross and Bob Hughes in a Japanese prison camp, Bob never to return. Old Mr Penny, who ran our little sweet shop on the corner fought back his tears as he warmly welcomed me. His only son, a flying officer, had been shot down over Germany and he bravely struggled to carry on in spite of his grief. Our once neat little road with happy families had taken a battering over the years and even our handsome wrought iron gates and railings had been removed to melt down for weapons of war. Sitting at the corner where he had played childhood games, my thoughts went back to "Jacko the Bookie" who would take illegal bets from the local people. My friend and I would get sixpence each from him to watch out for the police and when we waved he would hide his book and shelter in someone's house. It was always a running battle with the bookmakers and the Law, but great fun for the kids to watch.

Another character was "Tich", with a barrel organ, who had to stand on a box and twirl the handle. A tiny man with a large hat and a black moustache, who in spite of his size trundled around Fulham with a team of male dancers dressed in women's clothes, giving a wonderful song and dance show for just a few pennies. Jobs were scarce in the late twenties and it provided some sort of income for them.

After two weeks at home, I felt that I wanted to get back to military life and was pleased when I received a posting to Northumberland for a medical check. It was typical of the military to send me nearly three hundred miles when the Royal Artillery barracks were at Woolwich but it was good to be on the move once again. At Newcastle, I joined a group of ex-prisoners from various regiments from various regiments and several of my companions were paratroopers who had seen heavy fighting in Holland and Germany. As we formed up naked for the medical officer, his orderly referred to us as "The Thin White Line".

We had a quick physical check, followed by a few tasks to assess our mental state, which involved assembling a bicycle pump, a single lock and fitting shapes into their correct pockets. After a few easy sums, we were pronounced fit and normal. Physically fit perhaps but I was not too happy about our mental state. We all appeared to be in a state of delayed shock that had just began to emerge. The tight lips and taught faces under the red berets seemed to be an indication of the inner torment behind the façade of ribald humour which always surfaced on occasions like this. No doubt the passing years would dull the keen edge of the poignant memory, but mental scars would never be completely erased. Many years ahead, words and deeds would be recalled as though they took place only yesterday. Most of these present had a far away look in their eyes, as though searching through past experiences. Boys had gone into battle, men had returned.

After soldiering on for another twelve months with a training battery at Newcastle and enjoying every moment of the outdoor activity, my turn came for demob with a group of twenty-five men. Although we were offered a payment of two hundred pounds to extend our service, I decided to return to civilian life and try to carve out some sort of career for myself In the post war scramble for jobs. However, I knew that it would not be easy to settle down once again after the action of the past few years.

With a group of Londoners, I was sent to Olympia that was being used as a clothing depot for our transition from soldier to civilian. We were ushered into the melting pot of trilbys and tape measures and the fragrance of new clothing to flow smoothly along to collect our suits and shoes and raincoats and hats to emerge as fully fashioned civilians.

Looking round at the mixed group of men of whom I felt proud to be a part, I knew I would miss the comradeship of service life with the "long and the short and the tall". Behind the lean brown faces under bush hats worn by the jungle fighters and the berets of the paratroopers lurked a wealth of untold stories of heroism and drama, comedy and perhaps even love. Maybe there had been a tender encounter in some distant land. These were stories that would some day unfold and I knew that the haven I had found in the mountains of Italy with its genteel people would never be far from my thoughts.

As we changed from rough khaki to soft wool suits, gone were the proud campaign ribbons of Africa and Burma, Italy and Germany. Gone the chevrons and regimental badges; gone the bombardiers and corporals, the gunners and the privates. As we donned our faceless mufti, we grinned self consciously in lumberjack shirts and new shoes, hardly daring to set foot into a world where we would have to live with our own decisions, right or wrong, without the daily routine set out for us. We knew it would be a difficult time. Only our memories could not be handed to the quartermaster stores. I took my army great-coat and after dying it to navy blue, it served me well through many winters.

As the newly formed civilian army files through the exit, a fleet of taxicabs was lined up and I travelled in style on the February day to my home in Fulham. The little house was deserted and quiet. The old clock that my father would wind every week with loving care had ceased to swing and as I opened the door to the garden, a ginger cat jumped from the fence and sauntered casually in. I called him "Blitz" and he stayed for several months, patiently waiting for me to return in the evenings after I had resumed my career at the old firm.

My army gratuity was saved until I was able to obtain a visa and a passport and I boarded the train for Italy. I returned to the little village in the mountains for what I had hoped would be a happy reunion, only to find sadness and heartache. Motherly little Rosa greeted me with tears in her eyes and turned away unable to speak. Tina led me to the garden to break the sad news that her father Pino had died after a short illness. Her young brother who had been sent to an uncle in California when the war clouds began to gather had enlisted with the US army and had lost his life in Normandy. The once happy family had been devastated. Pino had never recovered from the blow. I reflected on the irony of it all and the sad parallel to my own family circumstances. Looking into the outhouse where we had brewed alcohol, I recalled how we had laughed and joked as the wood smoke billowed around us and we threw a glass of liquor into the flames to test the strength. Tina whose silvery voice would ring through the village was quiet and pensive. She said that they had prayed for me after I had left to join the partisans. The military authorities had informed them of my safe return.

I called on the priest who had given up his bed and provided me with a meal and together, we visited the cemetery to see Pino's resting place. After saying my farewells to the villagers, I proceeded to the mountain stronghold where I had stayed with the partisans and sat in the deserted cottage that had been our headquarters and the barns where we had spent so many nights. There were a few pieces of equipment laying around and names scrawled on the walls as a reminder of what had been.

The men who had defied the Nazis and Fascists in the fight for liberty, in spite of privation and terrible retribution were now just a part of our history but they had savoured the "Scent of Freedom".

Arrivederci